D1566490

FOLK TALE PLAYS
for
PUPPETS

FOLK TALE PLAYS
for
PUPPETS

13 royalty-free plays
for hand puppets,
rod puppets or marionettes

by
LEWIS MAHLMANN

AND

DAVID CADWALADER JONES

Publishers   PLAYS, INC.   *Boston*

Copyright © 1980 by

LEWIS MAHLMANN AND DAVID CADWALADER JONES

All rights reserved

CAUTION

NOTICE FOR AMATEUR PRODUCTION

NOTICE FOR PROFESSIONAL PRODUCTION

Mahlmann, Lewis
Folk tale plays for puppets.

CONTENTS: The rabbit who wanted red wings.—Perez and Martina.—The blue willow.—Toads and diamonds. [etc.]
1. Puppets and puppet-plays. 2. Tales—Juvenile drama. 3. Children's plays, American. [1. Puppets and puppet-plays. 2. Folklore. 3. Plays]
I. Jones, David Cadwalader, joint author. II. Title.
PN1980.M34   791.5'38   80-15451
ISBN 0-8238-0242-6

MANUFACTURED IN THE UNITED STATES OF AMERICA

Contents

Preface

This book is the third in our series of puppet plays. We felt this time we should put the accent on the folk tale, and have selected for adaptation representative tales from a wide variety of countries. The plays may be successfully performed with hand or rod puppets or marionettes, or they may be adapted for production by live actors, or a combination of both.

The puppet theater is a magical, wonderful world of make-believe. All ages can enjoy this thrilling experience of theater.

LEWIS MAHLMANN
DAVID CADWALADER JONES

Foreword

Folk tales tell about the nature and doings of the people who handed them down, and thus are a reflection, a mirror, for us.

Children would rather learn through play and laughter. As who would not? Puppeteers take pleasure in bringing the written and spoken word to life; in telling tales through pictures. Puppets possess the ability to assume the intended character perfectly, be it person, animal, or animated object. The puppeteer breathes life into them, speaks for them, and through them expresses what the part demands. The spectator concentrates on the puppet and is thus quickly captivated by the action.

Children expect justice. They expect a good deed to be appreciated; they are eager to help; but they also insist that the evil-doer be punished or be brought to recognize his evil ways. Children are forever ready for pranks and adventures. The realm of fantasy and fairy tales is as real to them as the potentialities of the present. In more than thirty years of puppeteering for children, I have come to the conviction that next to their love of adventure and pleasure, they most want to say what is in their hearts.

Lewis Mahlmann and David C. Jones are familiar with children's thoughts and feelings. In their books *Puppet Plays for Young Players* and *Puppet Plays from Favorite Stories*, they have worked up a great many fairy tales, arranging them as puppet plays in a format easily executed by both adults and children. The merry, interesting, and informa-

tive puppet plays in this book cannot but enhance the joy
of putting them on stage.

Playing is one of man's most basic needs. Accept the
offer of the authors, and treat yourself to the merriment
and satisfaction of a puppet play.

—GISELA LOHMANN

German Puppeteer and Secretary-General
U.N.I.M.A., West Germany (*Union Internationale
de la Marionette*)

FOLK TALE PLAYS
for
PUPPETS

THE GINGERBREAD BOY

A folk tale of old England

Characters

THE LITTLE OLD WOMAN
THE LITTLE OLD MAN
THE GINGERBREAD BOY
COW
CHICKS
HORSE
FARMER JONES
RED HEN
FOX
NARRATOR

SCENE 1

SETTING: *The kitchen of The Little Old Woman, with a window, center stage and stove at left.*
AT RISE: THE LITTLE OLD WOMAN *is looking out the window.* THE LITTLE OLD MAN *enters.*

NARRATOR: Once upon a time there lived a little old woman and a little old man. They hadn't any little boy or girl of their own, so they lived in a little old house all alone.

OLD MAN: Good morning, wife. It is such a beautiful day!

OLD WOMAN: It is a nice day, dear husband, but I feel sad.

OLD MAN: What's wrong, dear? I would think you would be happy when the sun shines like this.

OLD WOMAN: I don't have any little boy or girl to take care of, and that makes me unhappy and lonesome.

OLD MAN: Why don't you busy yourself with baking? You love to bake!

OLD WOMAN: What a good idea! (*Suddenly*) I know! I will bake a gingerbread boy.

OLD MAN (*Teasing*): Wouldn't it be a surprise if he came to life?

OLD WOMAN (*Earnestly*): Do you think it could happen? (*Laughs*) Oh, don't talk nonsense.

OLD MAN (*Laughing*): You never can tell what will happen. I'm going to read my paper. I'll be nearby if you need me.

OLD WOMAN: Good. I will start baking right away. I'll call you when I'm done. (OLD MAN *exits, laughing.*) Now I'll get ready to bake. (*She goes to table.*) Here's the cookie dough. First I must roll it out. (*Gets rolling pin*) Hm-m-m. (*She hums as she moves rolling pin.*) Now I'll cut it into the shape of a gingerbread boy. (*Hums again, gets cookie cutter*) Oh, how cute! Good! Here are currants for buttons. (*Pretends to put decorations on cookie*) One! Two! Three! Four! Five! Then two fat raisins for eyes. One! Two! Why, they twinkle! I'll make him a mouth of pink frosting. (*Gets tube of icing*) And a little peaked cap of white frosting. There! Now I'll pinch his little gingerbread nose and ears into shape. (*She bends over table.*) All done! (GINGERBREAD BOY *appears and she holds it up.*) Now we'll have a little gingerbread boy all our own. (*She opens door to oven.*) I'll pop him into the oven, like this. It won't be long till he's done. (*She puts* GINGERBREAD BOY *into oven, closes door, and cleans the table as she sings "London Bridge," or another merry tune, and she continues to hum this melody as she finishes cleaning up.*)

NARRATOR: And while the old woman cleaned her house the Gingerbread Boy baked until he was nice and brown. Then he grew hot! Oh, so hot!

GINGERBREAD BOY (*From inside oven*): Let me out! Let me out, Old Woman!

OLD WOMAN: Goodness gracious! Who is that? (*Sniffs*) It smells as if the Gingerbread Boy is done. I'd better take him out. (*Calls*) Husband! It's time! (OLD MAN *enters.*)

OLD MAN: Is the Gingerbread Boy ready?

OLD WOMAN (*Opening the oven door*): Look! (GINGERBREAD BOY *appears as she pretends to take him out of oven.*)

OLD MAN: Isn't he a nice one!

GINGERBREAD BOY: Nice one! I'm a nice one! Ha, ha!

OLD WOMAN: Why, he's alive! He's moving. Hold still, Gingerbread Boy. (*He jumps out of her hands and runs around the room.*)

OLD MAN: Come back, Gingerbread Boy! (OLD MAN *and* OLD WOMAN *chase* GINGERBREAD BOY *around the room.*)

GINGERBREAD BOY:
> Run! Run! Run! As fast as you can!
> You can't catch me. I'm the Gingerbread
> Man.

(*Exits*)

OLD MAN *and* OLD WOMAN (*Together*): Come back! Come back! (*They exit after him, on the run. Curtain*)

*   *   *

SCENE 2

SETTING: *A pasture.*

AT RISE: COW *is grazing, and* GINGERBREAD BOY *runs in.*

NARRATOR: And they couldn't catch him. So the Gingerbread Boy ran on and on. Soon he came to a cow in a pasture.

COW (*Sniffing*): Um! Um! (*Sniffs*) Stop, little Gingerbread Boy! I would like to eat you. Mooooo!

GINGERBREAD BOY:

> I've run away from a little old woman;
> I've run away from a little old man;
> And I can run away from you, I can.

(COW *chases* GINGERBREAD BOY.)

COW: Come here! Come here!

GINGERBREAD BOY:

> Run! Run! Run! As fast as you can!
> You can't catch me. I'm the Gingerbread
> Man. I am! I am!

COW (*Out of breath*): Oh, dear . . . I'd better stop, or all my milk will turn to butter. (*Calls out*) You're a naughty boy to run away from your parents! You'll be sorry! (COW *exits.*)

NARRATOR: And so the little Gingerbread Boy ran on and on. Soon he came to a horse. (HORSE *enters.*)

HORSE: Hi there, Gingerbread Boy.

GINGERBREAD BOY: No time! I'm in a hurry!

HORSE: Please stop, little Gingerbread Boy. You look very good to eat.

GINGERBREAD BOY:

> I've run away from a little old woman;
> I've run away from a little old man;
> I've run away from a cow;
> And I can run away from you, I can.

HORSE: I'm as fast as the wind, so I'll catch you. (HORSE *chases* GINGERBREAD BOY.)

NARRATOR: So the horse ran after him. They both ran as fast as the wind, but the Gingerbread Boy was faster.

GINGERBREAD BOY:
> Run! Run! Run! As fast as you can!
> You can't catch me. I'm the Gingerbread
> Man. I am! I am!

HORSE: Neighhhh! You are right. (*Out of breath*) I can't catch you! I must be getting old. Oh, well. I'll go back to my oats. (HORSE *exits. Curtain*)

*   *   *

SCENE 3

SETTING: *A farm, with a barn, center stage, and a haystack.*
AT RISE: FARMER *is pitching hay.*

NARRATOR: By and by the Gingerbread Boy came to a barn where a farmer was pitching his hay.
FARMER (*Singing to the tune of "London Bridge"*):
> Pitch the hay and store the wheat,
> Pile it high, nice and neat,
> Milk the cows and mow the field,
> Like a farmer!

(*Speaks*) I've worked hard, and I'm hungry. (*Sees* GINGERBREAD BOY *run in*) There's a delicious-looking gingerbread boy! Yum, yum! He smells good! (*Calls to* GINGERBREAD BOY) Don't run so fast, little Gingerbread Boy! Gingerbread boys are made to eat!
GINGERBREAD BOY (*Laughing*):
> I've run away from a little old woman;
> I've run away from a little old man;
> I've run away from a cow;
> I've run away from a horse;
> And I can run away from you, I can, I can!

FARMER: I'll catch you with my pitchfork! (FARMER *chases* GINGERBREAD BOY.)

GINGERBREAD BOY:

> Run! Run! Run! As fast as you can!
> You can't catch me. I'm the Gingerbread
> Man. I am! I am!

FARMER: Come back. Come back! (*Stops to catch his breath*) He's too fast for me. Guess I'll go back to my hay! Maybe my wife will have gingerbread for dessert tonight! (*He exits.*)

GINGERBREAD BOY: Ha, ha! (*Laughs, runs around the stage, and exits.*)

HEN (*Entering*): Cluck! Cluck! Farmer! Farmer! Where's my corn? I'm hungry! Cluck! Cluck! I am so hungry I could eat anything! (*She pecks around the stage and clucks.* GINGERBREAD BOY *enters.*)

GINGERBREAD BOY: Ha, ha!

HEN: Gingerbread Boy! Stand still a minute. I want to peck and nibble you. You look good, oh, so good to eat!

GINGERBREAD BOY:

> I've run away from a little old woman;
> I've run away from a little old man;
> I've run away from a cow;
> I've run away from a horse;
> I've run away from the farmer;
> And I can run away from you, I can, I can!

HEN: I'll catch you and feed you to my chicks. (HEN *chases* GINGERBREAD BOY, *clucking.* GINGERBREAD BOY *runs off and exits.* HEN *stops, out of breath.*) I'd better stop. I won't be able to lay any eggs. Cluck! Cluck! I'd better call my chicks and gather them together. Here, chick, chick, chick! (CHICKS *come running in.*)

CHICKS: Peep, peep!

HEN: We'll have nothing but chicken feed for dinner, I fear. Come along, now. (HEN *and* CHICKS *exit with much peeping and clucking. Curtain*)

*   *   *

SCENE 4

SETTING: *The river.*
AT RISE: *The* FOX *is on the bank.*

FOX: They say that I am a sly old fox. You can't keep me out of your chicken coops with any old fences or locks. I steal and lie and you can't trust me. You'll see that I am always on the hunt for something to eat. Watch your step and don't come too close. (*Laughs*) Ha, ha . . . I'm a hungry fox!
GINGERBREAD BOY (*Entering; alarmed*): Oh, oh! There's a fox. (*Calls out*)
   Run! Run! Run! Catch me if you can!
   You can't catch me. I'm the Gingerbread
   Man. I am! I am!
FOX: Hi, there, little Gingerbread Boy.
GINGERBREAD BOY:
   I've run away from a little old woman;
   I've run away from a little old man;
   I've run away from a cow;
   I've run away from a horse;
   I've run away from a farmer;
   I've run away from a hen;
   And I can run away from you, I can, I can!
FOX (*Bored*): Why, I wouldn't catch you if I could.
GINGERBREAD BOY (*Surprised*): You wouldn't?

Fox (*Slyly*): Oh, no! I don't like gingerbread.

Gingerbread Boy: Then maybe you can help me. I've got to cross this river. Everyone is chasing me. If I swam this river I would melt away, frosting cap and all.

Fox: Jump on my tail and I will take you across.

Gingerbread Boy: That's good of you. (*He jumps on* Fox's *tail and* Fox *pretends to swim behind the cut-out of the waves.* NOTE: *Use circular as well as up-and-down movements of the puppet. Hold the* Gingerbread Boy *on top of the* Fox *at the various places as mentioned in the following dialogue.*)

Fox: I think you had better get on my back or you may fall off.

Gingerbread Boy: Yes, I will! (*Moves to* Fox's *back*)

Fox: The water is deeper. You may get wet where you are. Jump on my neck.

Gingerbread Boy: All right! (*Jumps to* Fox's *neck*)

Fox: The water grows deeper still. Jump on my nose! Jump on my nose!

Gingerbread Boy: Sure enough! (*Moves to sit on nose of* Fox)

Fox (*Slyly*): Soon you'll be inside me, for now, I am going to eat you up!

Gingerbread Boy: Why, I thought you didn't like gingerbread boys.

Fox: You shouldn't believe everything you hear—especially from a fox!

Gingerbread Boy: Well, you won't eat me if I can help it. I'll tickle your nose. Tickle, tickle! (*Tickles nose of* Fox)

Fox: Stop! Don't do that! I'm going to sneeze if you do. I can't help it. Ah—ah—choo! (Gingerbread Boy *flies up into air and lands on the shore.*)

Gingerbread Boy: I'm safe on the shore.

Fox (*Floundering in the water*): Come back! Come back!
Gingerbread Boy: I've run away from everyone and I can run away from you. You can't catch me. And you won't eat me!
Fox (*Climbing onto the shore*): Come back! (Fox *chases* Gingerbread Boy.)
Narrator: But the little Gingerbread Boy ran all the way home. (Gingerbread Boy *exits with* Fox *in pursuit. Curtain.*)

*   *   *

Scene 5

Setting: *Same as Scene 1.*
At Rise: Old Woman *and* Old Man *are onstage.*

Old Woman: My little Gingerbread Boy has run away. Poor thing! (*Weeps*)
Old Man: Don't be sad. You can bake another gingerbread boy.
Old Woman: No, it wouldn't be the same.
Gingerbread Boy (*Running in*): Look! I've come home!
Old Woman: My little Gingerbread Boy! (Old Woman *embraces* Gingerbread Boy.)
Narrator: And so the Gingerbread Boy learned his lesson . . . as all good little boys and girls should . . . and he never ran away from home again. (*Curtain*)

THE END

The Gingerbread Boy

PRODUCTION NOTES

Number of Puppets: 8 hand or rod puppets or marionettes; several chicks (as many as desired) on multiple controls.

Playing Time: 15 minutes.

Costumes: The Little Old Woman wears a dress and an apron and has a mobcap on her head. The Little Old Man can be in his shirtsleeves with suspenders holding up his pants. The Farmer is in overalls with a plaid shirt and straw hat. The animals should be large, and constructed to move well. The Gingerbread Boy may be made with hinged joints, like a jumping jack, so that his arms and legs fold out. Paint a broad smile on his face.

Properties: Stove, with a swinging door; rolling pin; cookie cutter; tube of icing; newspaper (attached to the Little Old Man's hand); pitchfork (Farmer holds this in both hands).

Setting: Kitchen, a painted set on a drop, or, a cut-out, placed in front of the pasture drop. The farmyard scene shows the barn, and the haystack, painted on the drop (or make the haystack separately and put it in front of the stage). Show the river using a cut-out of waves, with an indication of shore on either end.

Lighting: No special effects.

Sound: No special effects; background music may be traditional English melodies, such as, "Country Gardens."

BABA YAGA

Traditional Russian folk tale

Characters

MARUSKA, *a pretty girl*
MOTHER
BABA YAGA, *the evil witch*
HEDGEHOG
CZAR
SOLDIER
PRINCE

SCENE 1

SETTING: *Outside Maruska's cottage in the woods. Flowers are growing near cottage.*
AT RISE: MOTHER *enters, carrying basket.*

MOTHER (*Calling*): Maruska! Maruska! Where are you? (MARUSKA *enters.*) Oh, there you are, Maruska. I'm afraid I won't have time to do the marketing today. (*Handing* MARUSKA *basket*) Take this basket and fill it with mushrooms at the village market for our dinner tonight.
MARUSKA: Yes, Mother. I'd be happy to do that for you.
MOTHER: And, Maruska—remember to stay away from the center of the forest, for that is where the evil witch, Baba Yaga, is said to dwell.
MARUSKA: Is Baba Yaga really an evil witch, Mother?
MOTHER: Oh, my, yes! They say she has a terrible tem-

per—and when she becomes hungry she roams through the forest searching for bad children to cook in her stew.

MARUSKA: That's so frightening! But how will I recognize her?

MOTHER: Baba Yaga lives in an old hut set on two immense chicken legs. She is very old, and she has long, wild hair and a large, pointed nose that she uses to sniff out bad children.

MARUSKA: I will certainly stay away from her!

MOTHER: Now, now. You have nothing to fear, so long as you are good. (*Hands coin to* MARUSKA) Here is the money for the mushrooms. Don't lose it. It is our last ruble, and the change must last us all week.

MARUSKA: I'll be careful with it, Mother. Goodbye. (*She kisses* MOTHER. MOTHER *exits.*) What a lovely day! And look at all these beautiful flowers. I'll pick some for Mother, and make her a bouquet. (*She picks flowers.*) There! Now, I must go to the village for the mushrooms. (*Pauses*) Where did I put that ruble? (*Searches; alarmed*) Oh, no! It's not in my pocket. I must have lost it! Oh, I've been very bad. Instead of picking flowers, I should have gone straight to the market. (*She weeps. A hut on chicken legs appears, and* BABA YAGA *jumps out of it.*)

BABA YAGA (*In threatening tone*): Bad? Bad? Did I hear someone say bad? (*Points to* MARUSKA) Why, it is a bad little Russian girl! Just what I need for my stew.

MARUSKA (*Backing away*): Stay away from me, you nasty old witch!

BABA YAGA: You're even more wicked than I thought— calling me names. You should really make a tasty stew. (*Grabs* MARUSKA)

MARUSKA (*Struggling*): Let me go! Let me go!

BABA YAGA: Don't waste time screaming and struggling. Once old Baba Yaga gets her bony hands on bad little girls, they never get away. (*Cackles*) Heh, heh, heh! Into the house with you! (*She jumps into hut, holding* MARUSKA, *and hut jumps offstage. Curtain*)

*   *   *

SCENE 2

SETTING: *Inside Baba Yaga's hut. Window, cupboard, with broom and dust cloth, cage, and stove, with stewpot, are at center stage.*
AT RISE: BABA YAGA *is stirring a pot of stew.* MARUSKA *is inside cage.*

BABA YAGA: A little salt, some fish heads, rats' tails, and a potato or two—there! That should give some flavor to my stew.
MARUSKA (*Crying out*): Let me out of here! I want to go home!
BABA YAGA: Quiet, little girl. Can't you see I'm busy?
MARUSKA: I can't move! Please let me out!
BABA YAGA: Oh, very well. You can't escape. Besides, you can do my housework while the stew boils. (*She opens cage and lets* MARUSKA *out.*) Now, sweep the floor, wash the dishes, and make me some tea.
MARUSKA: Yes, ma'am. (MARUSKA *gets broom and starts sweeping floor.*)
BAGA YAGA: When you finish all that, dust off the bottles in the cupboard. Now, where was I? Oh, yes. The stew. Well, a few withered berries, some bats' wings, and more salt. In a few hours, it will be ready (*Pointing to* MARUSKA) for its main ingredient. (*Wicked laugh*) Heh, heh, heh! (*Sound of horse's hoofs is heard from offstage.* MARUSKA *rushes to window.*)

MARUSKA: There is a horseman outside dressed all in black. He's riding a black horse. (*Pauses*) He's gone now. Who is he, Baba Yaga?

BABA YAGA: Questions, questions! Don't ask so many questions. Every time a child asks me a question, I grow ten years older. Didn't you know that?

MARUSKA: No, I didn't.

BABA YAGA: Well, you do now. I'll overlook it this time, but I will allow you to ask me only two more questions. So use them wisely. As for your first question—that horseman you saw was once my obedient servant, Moonless Knight.

MARUSKA: I wonder why he was dressed all in black.

BABA YAGA: Is that your second question? (*Cackles*) Heh, heh, heh!

MARUSKA (*Quickly*): No, no! I was just wondering out loud.

BABA YAGA: Be careful, or you'll use up your two questions before you know it.

MARUSKA: I don't want to do that!

BABA YAGA: Then, instead of standing there, grab that dust cloth and dust off those jars in the cupboard. (MARUSKA *gets dust cloth and goes to cupboard.*)

MARUSKA: What a lot of interesting jars! A jar of chicken legs, and one of spiders, and another with roots and herbs.

BABA YAGA: Yes! And they are all filled except for that one jar. (*Points*) When I fill that jar, I will be able to perform any evil magic, or break any magic spell, that I wish.

MARUSKA: I see. What do you need to fill up that jar?

BABA YAGA: A-ha! That was your second question. You have only one left.

MARUSKA: Oh, dear! I must be more careful.

BABA YAGA: I need the petals of a black moonflower to fill that jar—but I have not been able to locate any, though I have looked high and low. (*Weeps*)

MARUSKA: Don't cry, poor witch.

BABA YAGA (*Nastily*): Oh, be quiet! Get back into that cage. I am going out for a few minutes to see if I have caught any tasty squirrels or rabbits in my traps. They will give body to my stew—you look awfully scrawny to me. (BABA YAGA *puts* MARUSKA *into cage and exits.*)

MARUSKA (*Weeping*): Oh, me! What is to become of me? My poor mother must be so worried because I didn't come home last night.

BABA YAGA (*Re-entering*): Bah! Bad luck. (*Holds up* HEDGE-HOG) Nothing but this skinny hedgehog in my traps. Here. (*Throws* HEDGEHOG *into room and releases* MARUSKA *from cage*) He can keep you company, Maruska, while I go to the broom-maker's shop. Get out some onions, and make sure they are all peeled before I return. (*Exits*)

MARUSKA: Poor little hedgehog! Now you are a prisoner of Baba Yaga, too.

HEDGEHOG: Do not cry, Maruska. Perhaps the two of us can help each other.

MARUSKA (*Amazed*): Why, you can talk! How does it happen that you can speak?

HEDGEHOG: It is a very long story. Would you care to hear it?

MARUSKA: Yes, please. We have plenty of time.

HEDGEHOG: Very well. Sit here by me, and I will tell you the story. (MARUSKA *sits near* HEDGEHOG.) Many years ago, in a beautiful palace not far from here, lived a Czar and Czarina. They were very wealthy, but they had no children, and were lonely. Then, one day, in the palace garden, a beautiful flower bloomed mysteriously. Often, the Czar would sit in his garden and admire it. (*Curtain*)

*   *   *

S<small>CENE</small> 3

T<small>IME</small>: *Many years earlier.*
S<small>ETTING</small>: *The garden of the Czar. Part of the palace is seen at one side. There is a black flower at center stage.*
A<small>T</small> R<small>ISE</small>: *The* C<small>ZAR</small> *is walking in the garden.*

C<small>ZAR</small>: I am fortunate, indeed, to be Czar of all the land, and to have such a kind and beautiful wife—and so many precious gems and rubles. But, alas, I am not happy. If only I could have a child—even—even a child no bigger than a hedgehog. (*Flower shakes, and a tinkling sound is heard.*)
S<small>OLDIER</small> (*Entering*): Your Majesty! I have some news for you.
C<small>ZAR</small>: What is it, soldier?
S<small>OLDIER</small>: You have become a father.
C<small>ZAR</small>: What? (*Joyously*) What wonderful news. At last. Tell me—is it a boy or a girl?
S<small>OLDIER</small>: Well—ah—er—neither, Your Majesty.
C<small>ZAR</small>: What do you mean?
S<small>OLDIER</small>: The witch Baba Yaga cast an evil spell on your son as soon as it was born—and it turned into a—a—
C<small>ZAR</small> (*Anxiously*): Out with it! A what?
S<small>OLDIER</small>: A hedgehog, Your Majesty.
C<small>ZAR</small> (*Outraged*): Can this be true?
S<small>OLDIER</small>: Yes, Your Highness.
C<small>ZAR</small>: Perhaps somehow Baba Yaga's evil spell can be broken. Meanwhile, our hedgehog will be well taken

care of. Get him the best food and clothing, and hire learned tutors for his education.

SOLDIER: Yes, Your Majesty. (*Exits*)

CZAR: There must be a way to break the spell, so that someday my son may sit on the throne and rule the country.

SOLDIER (*Hurrying in*): Your Majesty, it is just as I feared. When the people heard about the hedgehog, they began to laugh. Their laughter is getting louder each hour. You must do something.

CZAR: The people are laughing, you say? The Czar cannot be laughed at. I fear there is nothing to do but banish the little hedgehog to the forest. Tell the people he has died of influenza.

SOLDIER: Yes, Your Majesty. As you wish. (*Exits. Curtain*)

*   *   *

SCENE 4

SETTING: *Same as Scene 2.*

AT RISE: HEDGEHOG *is telling his tale to* MARUSKA.

HEDGEHOG: Since I was banished many years ago, I have found life as a wild hedgehog very difficult. I was meant to live in a palace—in the forest, I barely have enough to eat.

MARUSKA: Poor little hedgehog! How miserable you must be.

HEDGEHOG: It cheers me to be able to speak with someone. I cannot understand the voices of the animals in the forest.

MARUSKA: Tell me more about this flower that you spoke of—the flower that grew in the Czar's garden.

HEDGEHOG: It is a moonflower, but not like other moon-flowers. This one is black.

MARUSKA: Black! Why, Baba Yaga has been searching all of Russia for such a black flower. Where is the Czar's palace?

HEDGEHOG: On the north edge of the forest—across the river and at the foot of a mountain. (*Sound of footsteps is heard from offstage.*)

MARUSKA: Oh-oh! I think I hear Baba Yaga at the door. Quickly, get into the cage. (MARUSKA *puts* HEDGEHOG *into cage.*)

BABA YAGA (*Entering*): What's all this chattering about, Maruska? Why aren't those onions peeled?

MARUSKA: I don't intend to peel the onions, or do any other work for you.

BABA YAGA: How dare you defy me, you wicked girl! But then, you'll soon be in the stewpot.

MARUSKA: I don't think you'll put me in the stew when you know my secret.

BABA YAGA: Secret? What secret? You can't put me off! Back to your work. I'm getting hungry.

MARUSKA: Suppose I could tell you where the black moon-flower grows?

BABA YAGA (*Excited; going to* MARUSKA, *grabbing her and shaking her*): You can't know that! Tell me, or I'll—

MARUSKA: I'll tell you if you will give me some mush-rooms, for my mother.

BABA YAGA: Here—help yourself—fill your basket. (*Gets mushrooms, hands them to* MARUSKA) Only tell me, where can the black moonflower be found?

MARUSKA (*Filling her basket*): If you follow me I will lead you to it.

BABA YAGA: Yes! Take your mushrooms and show me. Hurry! I must have that flower! (*As they start off*) Hurry! Walk faster! (BABA YAGA *pushes* MARUSKA *off. Curtain*)

*   *   *

SCENE 5

SETTING: *Czar's garden, as in Scene 3. Black flower is at center.* AT RISE: MARUSKA *and* BABA YAGA *enter.* MARUSKA *carries her basket of mushrooms.*

BABA YAGA (*Puffing*): Is it much farther? I haven't walked so far in centuries.
MARUSKA: We should be close to the Czar's palace by now.
BABA YAGA: We had better be. If this is a trick, I'll—
MARUSKA (*Pointing to flower*): There's the flower! Look. It's so beautiful.
BABA YAGA: It is! It is! It really is a black moonflower. Once I tear off its petals, I will be able to perform any evil magic, or break any spell, that I wish. (*Runs over to flower*)
MARUSKA: Oh, don't pick that beautiful flower! (*Rushes over to stand in front of flower, blocking* BABA YAGA's *arm*)
BABA YAGA (*Pushing* MARUSKA *aside*): Out of my way, silly child. (*Pulls on flower*) I must . . . pull this . . . (*Struggling*) Uh-h-h . . . .
MARUSKA: Wait! Baba Yaga?
BABA YAGA (*Cross*): What do you want? Make it quick— I'm in a hurry!
MARUSKA: I still have one more question to ask you, and I'd like to ask it now.

BABA YAGA: Oh, very well. What is it?

MARUSKA: Why did you think I was so bad that you should eat me in your stew?

BABA YAGA: Because you lost the money your mother gave you to buy mushrooms.

MARUSKA: But I have my mushrooms now, and I'm not bad anymore, so you can't eat me, can you?

BABA YAGA (*Sighing*): You may be right, but I can still eat that skinny hedgehog. Now, Maruska, go away! And don't bother me. (*Struggling to pull up flower again*) I must . . . pull up . . . this flower. (*Pulling at flower, which seems to hold her fast*) I'm stuck. I can't get away. My hands are stuck to the flower! Maruska, you must help me. Pull me off!

MARUSKA: Why? Are you stuck? What did you do? Do you expect me to help you? Why should I free you?

BABA YAGA: Stop! Stop! You are asking too many questions! I grow ten years older with each one!

MARUSKA: What's happening? What did I do? Should I get help? Whom can I call? Are you still stuck? What should I do?

BABA YAGA: Oh, stop! Stop! That's six questions, and sixty more years. Oh, I grow old too fast! You will be the death of me!

MARUSKA: Are you really getting older? You won't eat that poor little hedgehog, will you?

BABA YAGA (*Falling down*): Oh, this is the end. One question too many! Agh-h-h! (*She dies, sinking away behind stage.*)

MARUSKA: Oh, dear! Baba Yaga is dead. I had better go rescue the little hedgehog, because it is still inside her house. (*Calling*) Hedgehog! Hedgehog! I'm coming to rescue you! (*Just as she starts off,* PRINCE *enters.*) Why, who are you? And where is my hedgehog?

PRINCE: More questions? (*Laughs as he approaches* MARUSKA *and takes her hands*) I was the little hedgehog, sweet Maruska. When old Baba Yaga died, the spell she cast on me was broken, and I became a prince once again.

MARUSKA (*Amazed*): My hedgehog—a prince! Now you can return to your palace and rule your country.

PRINCE: Yes, and it is your doing. Thank you, Maruska. You are kind and good, and I want you to rule with me, as Queen. Please say you'll do me the honor of becoming my wife.

MARUSKA: One day, perhaps. But I am still much too young. I must take these mushrooms home to Mother now. She has been waiting two days for them!

PRINCE: I shall wait, dear friend. And I will remember you always, sweet Maruska. Goodbye!

MARUSKA: Goodbye. Goodbye, my hedgehog prince! (*They wave and she exits. Curtain*)

THE END

Baba Yaga

PRODUCTION NOTES

Number of Puppets: 7 hand or rod puppets or marionettes.

Playing Time: 25 minutes.

Costumes: Appropriate Russian period clothing. Maruska and her mother wear long dresses or blouses and skirts, with aprons. Mother wears a scarf on her head. Baba Yaga is in a long, tattered dress and shawl. Her head is bare and she has long, snarled gray hair. Czar is in a long, double-breasted coat; he wears a crown. Soldier and Prince are in bloomer-like pants, knee-length jackets and hats: a tall, smooth, brimless hat for the Soldier and a fur beret for the Prince.

Properties: Basket; coin; flowers; Baba Yaga's hut on chicken legs (a wooden cottage that has movable legs); dustcloth; pot of stew; cage; stove; broom.

Setting: The woods with Maruska's cottage, which is a low log cabin; interior of Baba Yaga's hut, which has a stove, a window, a cupboard, and a cage (paint on the background and on the stove the items Baba Yaga mentions); the Czar's garden, with the large, glittering black moonflower at center, surrounded by smaller, brightly-colored flowers, and with part of the Czar's palace of elaborately painted wood visible on one side.

Lighting: No special effects.

Sound: No special effects. A Russian composer's music, "Pictures at an Exhibition" by Mussorgsky, for example, may be used as background music.

THE LITTLE INDIAN BRAVE

A tale of the North American Indians

Characters

KEOKUK, *an Indian chief*
YUKI, *his grandson*
TATANGA MANI, *the medicine man*
WEST WIND, *a beautiful spirit*
OWL
BEAVER
BEAR
COYOTE
SPIDER
HAWK

SCENE 1

SETTING: *An Indian village. Teepee is at center. Brown, dry grasses are scattered about.*
AT RISE: GRANDFATHER *and* YUKI *are outside teepee.*

KEOKUK: Come closer, my child. You must listen carefully to what I have to say.
YUKI: Yes, Grandfather. (*Moves closer to* KEOKUK)
KEOKUK: I am an old man, and I have become very weak because of the great famine. I can no longer care for you. It is time for you to take your place among the braves.
YUKI: But, Grandfather, I don't think I am ready to become a brave.

KEOKUK: It must be so, Yuki. You are almost a man now, and you must try to equal your father in courage and skill.

YUKI: Very well. What must I do?

KEOKUK: You must perform three difficult deeds. If you succeed, the gods will reveal to you their secret, and you will become a brave!

YUKI: What if I fail?

KEOKUK: Then you will be driven from the tribe—and our family will be disgraced.

YUKI: Then I shall do my best to succeed. Do not worry, Grandfather. Tell me, what are these three deeds I must perform?

KEOKUK: That I cannot tell you. Only Tatanga Mani, the shaman, can tell you. Go to his cave in the mountains.

YUKI: It is a long journey. I shall leave at once.

KEOKUK: Be careful, Yuki, and remember to beware of Coyote—he is not to be trusted.

YUKI: I shall remember, Grandfather.

KEOKUK: Go now, Yuki. My blessings on you for a safe journey.

YUKI: Goodbye, Grandfather. Rest well. I shall not fail you. (YUKI *exits. Curtain*)

*   *   *

SCENE 2

SETTING: *A forest in the mountains. At center, there is a tree which has a spider web hanging from one branch.*

AT RISE: YUKI *enters.*

YUKI: What a long journey to the cave of Tatanga Mani! I must rest awhile. (*He sits under tree.*) Ho hum! (*Loud sounds of birds chirping are heard from offstage.*)

OWL (*From above*): Help! Someone, help me!

YUKI (*Jumping up*): What? Who was that? Who calls for help?

OWL (*Flying in*): Up here, little one. It is I, the Owl. Help me! Hawk is trying to steal my eggs.

YUKI: What a greedy Hawk! This stone will scare him. (*Pantomimes throwing stone*) Shoo! Shoo! Shoo, Hawk!

HAWK (*Appearing*): Caw! Caw! (*Flies off*)

OWL (*Flying down from tree*): Thank you, thank you! You have saved my eggs.

YUKI: I was happy to drive the Hawk away. But were you really speaking before?

OWL: Yes. All birds and animals can talk, but we speak only to those we trust.

YUKI: Does that mean you trust me?

OWL: Oh, my, yes. I have been watching you, and I know you are good. You are gentle and kind to others, and never mistreat those smaller or weaker than you.

YUKI: Thank you. Tell me, Owl—is it very far to Tatanga Mani's cave? I must go there to learn the three deeds I must perform.

OWL: It is not far, but the trip can be dangerous. Call on me if you need help—I shall not be far away. Goodbye, my friend.

YUKI: Goodbye, Owl. (OWL *flies off*.) Now, I'd better be on my way again. I'll need a walking stick. (*He goes to tree and breaks off branch with spider web on it.*) This one will do.

SPIDER (*Appearing*): Oh, no! Look what you've done! You broke my web and a juicy fat fly got away!

YUKI (*Looking all around*): Who said that?

SPIDER: I did. Look down here on the ground. It is I, Spider. When you broke that branch, you destroyed my beautiful web.

YUKI: I'm sorry, Spider. I didn't see the web. I'll put the

stick back, and you can spin another web in the same place. (*He leans stick against tree.*)

SPIDER: Why, thank you. You are very kind. If you ever need any help, just call on me.

YUKI: Thank you, Spider. I hope you will catch more flies in your web. I must be on my way now. Goodbye.

SPIDER: Goodbye, and good luck to you. (YUKI *exits. Curtain*)

*   *   *

SCENE 3

SETTING: *Outdoor area near Tatanga Mani's cave. Fallen log and branches lie on the ground. Cave opening is at one side.*

AT RISE: BEAVER *is onstage, partly hidden under the branches.* YUKI *enters.*

YUKI: At last! I can see the cave up ahead.

BEAVER: Ho, over there! Could you help me, please?

YUKI: Who is it? (*Seeing* BEAVER) Why, it's a beaver! What seems to be the matter?

BEAVER: I was gnawing branches to build my home by the river, and a large log fell on my tail. I can't move. Could you lift it off, please?

YUKI: I'll try. (*With much effort, he lifts log*) There! It's off!

BEAVER (*Coming out*): Thank you. I'm glad you came when you did! If you ever need any help, just let me know. I must finish building my home now. Goodbye. (*He exits.*)

YUKI: Goodbye. Now to find the shaman. (*Calls*) Hello! Is anybody there?

TATANGA MANI (*Appearing*): Who calls the great Tatanga Mani?

YUKI: It is I, Yuki, grandson of Keokuk the Indian chief.

TATANGA MANI: What is it you wish?

YUKI: Tell me the deeds I must perform in order to discover the great secret of the gods.

TATANGA MANI: Ah, for this you must be very courageous and strong. Do you think that you are ready to join the other braves of your tribe?

YUKI: I hope I am ready!

TATANGA MANI: Very well. I will tell you what you must do. First, to gain courage, you must get a tail feather from the Eagle.

YUKI: That sounds difficult, but I will try my best.

TATANGA MANI: Next, you must obtain a strip of fur from the Bear, which you will make into a belt. This will give you the strength you will need as a warrior.

YUKI: And what is the last deed?

TATANGA MANI: Finally, you must set the West Wind free. Coyote has stolen this beautiful spirit, who brings us the rain each year. You must release her so that our land will turn green again and your people will not starve.

YUKI: That I will do gladly—if I can.

TATANGA MANI: If you fail, Yuki, you know the consequences!

YUKI: Yes, Tatanga Mani. Many members of my tribe will die, and Grandfather will be disgraced. I must not fail!

TATANGA MANI: Well spoken, little one. Now, go. And may the Great Spirit watch over you. (YUKI *bows and exits.* TATANGA MANI *enters his cave. Curtain*)

*   *   *

SCENE 4

SETTING: *A cliff on the side of a mountain. An eagle is sleeping on nest at top of cliff.*

AT RISE: YUKI *is climbing the mountain.*

YUKI: I'm almost at the top of the mountain where the Eagle has his nest. (*Pauses and looks up*) Oh, no! Look at this steep ridge! How can I possibly climb it? No wonder the Eagle built his nest here. No one could ever reach it.

OWL (*Flying in*): I can fly to the Eagle's nest. Let me help you, Yuki.

YUKI (*Pleased*): Owl! Thank goodness you're here. I need to get a tail feather from the Eagle—if I wear the feather in my headband, I will have courage.

OWL: I think I know a way to get it for you. The Eagle is asleep now in his nest, and his tail is sticking out over the edge. I'll fly by it quickly, pull out a feather, and bring it back to you.

YUKI: You are so kind, Owl. (*Suddenly concerned*) Do you think the Great Spirit will be angry if I get help from you?

OWL: No, for you have shown great courage already in climbing this far up the mountain. Also, I want to repay you for your kindness to me in driving the Hawk away from my eggs. (OWL *flies off.*)

YUKI: I do hope Owl is successful. Then I will have only two more tasks to accomplish. (OWL *returns with feather.*)

OWL: Here is the feather.

YUKI (*Taking feather*): Thank you, Owl. You are indeed my friend.

OWL: Now, you must go quickly. The Eagle will be in a rage when he wakes up and finds his feather gone! (*They exit. Curtain*)

*   *   *

Scene 5

SETTING: *Beaver's home on a river bank. Many branches are piled up.*

At Rise: Yuki, *wearing eagle's feather in his headband, and* Beaver, *are onstage.*

Yuki: Now that I have the feather from the Eagle, I must find old Bear and get a strip of fur from his coat. That will give me strength to become a brave.

Beaver: Ay! You are fortunate. Old Bear comes to this very spot for a drink each day about this time.

Yuki: Good. (*Pauses, looking off*) I think I hear him approaching now.

Beaver: Quickly, then. Hide in my house and I will try to get a strip of his fur for you.

Yuki: Good Beaver, how kind you are!

Beaver: In the same way you were kind to me, Yuki. (Yuki *hides behind the branches.* Bear *enters.* Beaver *stands to one side.*)

Bear: Ho, hum. Now for a nice cool drink of water.

Beaver: Ho, there, Bear. How are you today?

Bear: Who speaks to Bear?

Beaver: It is I, Beaver.

Bear: Oh, yes. I see you now. My eyes are not what they used to be.

Beaver: You must have had a difficult journey today.

Bear: What makes you say that, Beaver?

Beaver: Because your coat is all covered with burrs and thorns.

Bear: I certainly hate to have my shiny coat all matted.

Beaver: Would you like me to pull off the thorns?

BEAR: That would be helpful. I can't reach my back. (BEAVER *pulls at* BEAR's *shaggy coat.*)

BEAVER: My, my. The thorns are stuck fast. I'll have to use my sharp teeth to get them off.

BEAR: That's all right. My hide is tough. (BEAVER *bends over* BEAR. *A ripping sound is heard.* BEAVER *pulls strip of fur from* BEAR's *back.*)

BEAVER: There! The burrs are off, but I'm afraid I've pulled off some of your fur, too.

BEAR: No matter. It will grow back again. Thank you, my friend. Now I must take my nap. Goodbye. (*He exits.*)

BEAVER: Good day, Bear. (*Calling*) Yuki! You can come out now. (YUKI *comes out from behind branches.*) Here is the strip of fur from Bear's coat, just as I promised.

YUKI: Thank you so much, Beaver. You are a true friend.

BEAVER: What I have done is little enough to repay you for saving my life.

YUKI: Now I've only one more deed to perform. Goodbye!

BEAVER: Be careful, Yuki. Goodbye. (YUKI *exits. Curtain*)

*   *   *

SCENE 6

SETTING: *Same as Scene 2; tall grass is standing at side.*

AT RISE: COYOTE *enters, carrying a large bag.* WEST WIND *is inside bag.*

WEST WIND (*From inside bag*): Coyote! Coyote! Let me out of this bag immediately. I have important work to do!

COYOTE: Quiet, you howling wind! You are my prisoner, and the Indians will have to pay me a large ransom to set you free. No matter how much you howl, I shall not release you from this bag. (YUKI *appears and hides behind tree. He wears fur belt.*)

WEST WIND (*From bag*): You must set me free. The people need the rain I shall blow over their lands. The Indians are starving!

COYOTE: Let them starve! They never feed me! Now be quiet, noisy wind. I want to rest. I shall lie down here for a minute. (*He falls asleep and snores.*)

YUKI (*Emerging*): Good—the Coyote is asleep. I must get the bag away from him, but how can I do it without waking him? I wish I had a net to cover him. If only I knew how to weave, I could weave this tall grass into a net.

SPIDER (*Appearing; calling softly*): Yuki!

YUKI: Little Spider! I am glad to see you.

SPIDER: I can show you how to weave, Yuki.

YUKI: You are a good friend, Spider. Quickly, let's begin. (SPIDER *and* YUKI *turn back to audience, bend over grasses as if weaving.*)

SPIDER: Just weave some this way.

YUKI: Like this?

SPIDER: Yes. Then this way.

YUKI: Why, this is easy!

SPIDER: Good boy. You learn fast.

YUKI: Thank you for teaching me to weave, Spider.

SPIDER: I am glad to teach you, because you were kind enough to help me rebuild my web. (*Goes to side. Grass is removed.* YUKI *holds up a net.*)

YUKI (*Displaying net*): There! The net is finished. I will throw it over Coyote. (*He creeps over to* COYOTE *and throws the net over him.*)

COYOTE (*Awakening*): What's this? What happened? (*Tries to get up and push away the net*) I'm caught in a net. Help, someone! Let me out!

YUKI: No, Coyote. I have come to release the West Wind, and I shall do so while you are caught in the net.

COYOTE (*Craftily*): Don't be foolish, Yuki. With the ransom I can get for West Wind from the Indians, we could both be rich.

YUKI (*Interested*): Rich? What could I have?

COYOTE: Whatever you want. The best set of bow and arrows in all the land, for instance.

YUKI (*Musing*): Hmmm—I could use a new bow.

COYOTE: And the largest tent—made only of the best skins—and a headdress with one thousand feathers.

YUKI: What a splendid sight that would be!

SPIDER: Psst! Yuki! Remember what your Grandfather said!

YUKI: You're right, Spider. Grandfather said Coyote was not to be trusted. (*Firmly, to* COYOTE) I will not listen to you, Coyote.

COYOTE: Don't be silly, boy!

YUKI: I will set West Wind free. And I will do it now! (*He opens bag and* WEST WIND *comes out, making noise of wind.*)

WEST WIND: Shhhhhhhhhhh! Thank you, Yuki. That took a lot of courage. You are a smart lad. You will not be sorry. Goodbye! Shhhhhhhhh! (*She flies off, pulling* COYOTE *behind her.*)

SPIDER: Look, Yuki! It is cloudy and windy already, and soon the rains will come, thanks to your bravery.

YUKI: I must get back to my tribe now, and tell Grandfather that I have accomplished the three deeds. Goodbye, dear Spider. And thank you for being such a good friend and teacher. (YUKI *exits. Curtain*)

*   *   *

SCENE 7

SETTING: *Same as Scene 1.*

AT RISE: YUKI *enters. The feather is no longer in his headband.*

YUKI (*Calling*): Grandfather! I'm home. (KEOKUK *enters.*)

KEOKUK: Yuki! Thank the Great Spirit, you are safe and well.

YUKI: Grandfather, the land is turning green again. The drought is over!

KEOKUK: Yes, my child. We are all grateful. Did you perform your three deeds?

YUKI: Yes, Grandfather, but I am afraid I failed one of them. When I released the West Wind from Coyote's bag, the Eagle's feather must have blown away. I could not find it. I cannot give it to Tatanga Mani. (*Sadly*) I guess I am not ready to become a brave after all.

KEOKUK: Wait. Tell me, in carrying out your deeds, did you learn the mystery of the Great Spirit?

YUKI (*Timidly*): I think I did, Grandfather.

KEOKUK: And what is that, my child?

YUKI: I learned that the Great Spirit created each bird, insect, animal and man with a special talent, and when we all live and work together peacefully and share our talents, any deed, no matter how difficult, is possible.

KEOKUK (*Happily*): Yuki, the Great Spirit has indeed given you his secret. You are no longer a child. You are a brave! (KEOKUK *picks up a full headdress of feathers and puts it on* YUKI's *head. Curtain*)

THE END

The Little Indian Brave

PRODUCTION NOTES

Number of Puppets: 10 hand or rod puppets, or marionettes.

Playing Time: 25 minutes.

Costumes: Yuki, Keokuk, and Tatanga Mani wear moccasins, fringed pants and shirts that are decorated with beads and colorful trimmings. Keokuk has a feather in his headband. Yuki's headband is plain. Tatanga Mani wears buffalo headdress with horns. West Wind wears long, flowing robes that blow about when she moves, and a headdress with many feathers. She has loose bag tied around her when she first appears. Animals wear appropriate costumes—Bear has fur strip pinned to back.

Properties: Feather, heavy net made to look like grass woven together, elaborate feather headdress.

Setting: Scenes 1 and 7: an Indian village, with teepee center stage. Dry, brown grasses are scattered about in Scene 1. Scene 2, a forest. There is a large tree with a loose branch, which should move like a hinge. Make a spider web of string, attaching it to the tree and to the loose branch. Scene 3, a cave with an opening. There should be branches and a log on stage. Scene 4, the side of a cliff. An eagle's nest with a sleeping eagle is on top. Scene 5, a river bank with Beaver's house. Scene 6, same as Scene 2, with tall grass, made of stiff paper, standing at one side. We suggest you cut the teepee, cave, tree, Beaver's house and cliff out of cardboard and back the cardboard with wood supports. Attach the grass to a stick at the bottom.

Lighting: No special effects.

Music: Recorded American Indian music, or if desired, use drums and kazoo.

THE TABLE, THE DONKEY AND THE STICK

Adapted from the German folk tale by the Brothers Grimm

Characters

FATHER, *a poor tailor*
JOHANN, *his older son*
KARL, *his younger son*
ANNA, *his daughter*
CARPENTER
INNKEEPER
WEAVER
DONKEY
NARRATOR

SCENE 1

SETTING: *The tailor's cottage, a room crowded with furniture.*

NARRATOR: There once was a poor tailor who had two sons and one daughter. They lived happily together in their little cottage, until one day the father spoke to his son, Johann.

FATHER: Johann, my son, we cannot go on much longer unless I find more work. The people in this village are poor and there is little for us to do here. I'm afraid I will have to sell our cottage unless one of us goes to the big city to earn some money.

JOHANN: I will go, Father. I will try to find work as a carpenter, for I am very good with tools.

FATHER: I was hoping you would say that, son, for I am too old to find another job.

JOHANN: Do not worry, Father. I will leave at once. I have nothing to pack. Say goodbye to Karl and Anna for me. I hate tearful farewells, and you know that Anna always weeps when she is sad. Goodbye, Father.

FATHER: Farewell, son. Come back home as soon as possible. (JOHANN *exits and* FATHER *follows him offstage.*)

NARRATOR: One year passed. (*Part of the furniture is removed.* FATHER *re-enters with* KARL *and* ANNA.)

FATHER: Ah, children. A whole year has passed since Johann left to seek his fortune, and still not a word from him. I am afraid your brother has failed and is too ashamed to return home.

ANNA: Do not fear, Father. Surely we will hear from Johann soon.

FATHER: Perhaps, Anna, but alas—business has not improved, and I can no longer afford to buy food for all of us.

KARL: Never fear, Father. I have decided that it is my turn to go to seek my fortune. I will try to get a job grooming horses on the King's estate. I hear they are looking for a new stable boy.

FATHER: Yes, Karl. That sounds like an excellent idea. Perhaps you will succeed where your poor brother has failed.

ANNA: Do not say that, Father. Johann will return. You'll see. And Karl will help us.

KARL: Yes. I'd better leave now, before someone else gets the stable boy's job.

FATHER: Goodbye, son, and good luck.

ANNA: Goodbye, Karl. (*She weeps.* KARL *exits.* FATHER *and* ANNA *follow him offstage.*)

NARRATOR: Another year passes. (*Most of the remaining furniture is removed.* FATHER *and* ANNA *re-enter.*)

FATHER: Oh, Anna, my daughter, what are we going to do? We have not heard a word from either of your brothers. We have sold most of the furniture and all of your late mother's beautiful dishes. And still I have barely enough money to buy food.

ANNA: Never mind, Father. I have made up my mind to go to the city and try my luck as a weaver in the tapestry factory.

FATHER: But, Anna, you are too young to go by yourself to the city.

ANNA: I am twenty-three, Father, and old enough to be able to take care of myself.

FATHER: Very well. Go, if you must, Anna. But write to me—and come to see me often.

ANNA: I will, Father. Don't worry. You must take care of yourself while I am gone. Goodbye.

FATHER: Goodbye, sweet Anna. Don't be like your brothers. (*She exits. Curtain.*)

*　　　*　　　*

SCENE 2

SETTING: *Carpenter's shop, with workbench onstage, holding wood and tools. Scene may be played in front of curtain.*

AT RISE: CARPENTER *and* JOHANN *are onstage.*

CARPENTER: You have worked for me as a carpenter's apprentice for two years, Johann. You have learned your trade very well.

JOHANN: Thank you, sir. I have tried to do my best.

CARPENTER: I have nothing else to teach you. It is time for you to go out on your own and open your own shop.

JOHANN: It makes me happy to hear that, sir. I am anxious to return home to my family.

CARPENTER: Before you leave, Johann, I would like to give you a token of my appreciation for your hard work. (*Gets table*)

JOHANN (*In surprise*): A table? (*Without enthusiasm*) Thank you, sir. That is kind of you.

CARPENTER: Do not look so disappointed. This is no ordinary, common table, I assure you.

JOHANN: What do you mean?

CARPENTER: This is a magic table. Watch. (*Recites*) "Table, be covered." (*The table is filled with food.*)

JOHANN (*Amazed*): Why, it is magic! The table was bare at first, but now it is covered with a tablecloth, and holds dishes of fine roast meat, and drink. It is truly amazing!

CARPENTER: This table will satisfy your needs for the rest of your life, Johann. Whenever you are hungry, all you have to say is, "Table, be covered," and you will have all the food you want.

JOHANN (*Excited*): Thank you. Thank you! Father will be pleased. He needed a way to find food for our family.

CARPENTER: Good. Now, be off with you. And good luck.

JOHANN: Goodbye, sir. And thank you. Thank you! (JOHANN *exits, with table. Curtain.*)

*   *   *

SCENE 3

SETTING: *In front of an inn.*

AT RISE: JOHANN *enters, carrying table.*

JOHANN: I think I will stop and rest at this inn before I go home to Father. This table is heavy. (INNKEEPER *comes out of the inn.*)

INNKEEPER: Good day, my friend. Can I offer you something to drink? You look tired and thirsty.

JOHANN: No—but I can offer you something. (*Recites*) "Table, be covered." (*Food appears on table.*)

INNKEEPER: Heavens! How did you do that?

JOHANN: It's a magic table. It will give me food whenever I command.

INNKEEPER: My! What a lucky fellow you are.

JOHANN: Yes. I'm taking the table home to my poor father. But I still have a long way to go, and I am tired.

INNKEEPER: Don't worry. I will let you stay here at my inn tonight free. Having such an important person here will be good for business.

JOHANN: Why, how kind of you.

INNKEEPER: It's nothing. Just follow me. I will give you my best room. (*Exits with* JOHANN, *then re-enters*) Ha! Good. He sleeps. Now I will take that magic table and put another in its place. Such a table will make my inn prosper. (*He switches tables, then exits. Lights dim, or curtains close briefly, to indicate passage of time. Sound of birds singing is heard.*)

JOHANN (*Entering with* INNKEEPER): Your room was comfortable, and the service excellent. How can I ever repay you?

INNKEEPER: Oh, you have, my young friend! You have. Just by staying here.

JOHANN: You're very kind. Well, I must be going now. I'll take my table, here, and be off. (*He lifts table.*) That's strange. It seems to be much lighter today.

INNKEEPER: That's because you had a good night's sleep and are not so tired.

JOHANN: Yes, perhaps you are right. Well, goodbye.
INNKEEPER: Farewell. (JOHANN *exits. Curtain.*)

*   *   *

SCENE 4

TIME: *The next day.*
SETTING: *The same as Scene 1. All the furniture is gone.*
AT RISE: JOHANN *enters, with table.*

JOHANN: Father! I'm home. It's Johann.
FATHER (*Entering*): Johann, my son! How good it is to see
   you! I had almost given you up for lost. Where have
   you been?
JOHANN: It's a long story, Father. But, look, look, what I
   have brought you!
FATHER: A table? How nice. This will be useful. I don't
   have any table or chairs now. I had to sell all the furni-
   ture.
JOHANN: This is not just an ordinary table, Father. It's a
   magic table.
FATHER: Magic? I don't believe it!
JOHANN: No? Well, watch. (*Recites*) "Table, be covered."
   (*Nothing happens.*)
FATHER: Well? Is something supposed to happen?
JOHANN: Wait. Maybe I didn't say it right. (*Shouts*)
   "Table, be covered."
FATHER: I'm waiting.
JOHANN (*Disappointed*): Oh, no! The magic must have worn
   off. (*Sadly*) I knew it was too good to be true.
FATHER: Don't look so sad, son. At least I have a table to
   eat on now, and best of all, I have you with me again.

JOHANN: I'm happy to be home, Father. (*They embrace. Curtain.*)

*   *   *

SCENE 5

SETTING: *Same as Scene 3.*
AT RISE: KARL *enters with* DONKEY.

KARL: I cannot believe my good luck. I have been away from home for only one year, and already I am the richest person in the kingdom . . . thanks to my magic donkey, here.

INNKEEPER (*Entering*): Welcome to my inn, young man. Did I hear you say that you had a magic donkey?

KARL: Yes, I did say that, Innkeeper. I have been working at the King's stables for one year and he liked my work so well that he gave me this magic donkey.

INNKEEPER (*Sneakily*): Ho! In what way is he magic?

KARL: I'll show you. Watch! All you have to do is pull his ear and say, ''Brickelbrit,'' and gold pours from his mouth.

INNKEEPER (*Greedily*): What are you waiting for? Do it! Do it!

KARL: Very well. (*He pulls* DONKEY's *ear.*) ''Brickelbrit.''

DONKEY: Hee-haw. (DONKEY's *mouth opens, and gold pieces pour out.*)

INNKEEPER: My, that is an easy way to get money! A donkey like that is a rare and wonderful gift.

KARL: Yes! I am taking it home to my poor father, so that he will never have to work again.

INNKEEPER: What a thoughtful son you are. But you look

tired. With all that money of yours, you should stay here for the night and rest. You can get off to a fresh start in the morning.

KARL: That's a fine idea. I'll take the best room in the inn. Here are some gold coins for you—please see that my donkey is fed and well cared for.

INNKEEPER: Oh, I'll take care of him, all right. Come, I'll show you to your room. (*They exit, leaving* DONKEY *on-stage.*)

DONKEY: Hee-haw.

INNKEEPER (*Re-entering*): Good! He's asleep. The fool! How could he be so trusting? I'll take his donkey and replace it with the one in my stable. He won't even know the difference. (*He leads* DONKEY *off, then enters leading another* DONKEY.) There! Now I will have all the gold I need. Ho, ho, ho! (*He exits. Lights dim to indicate passage of time. Sound of birds singing is heard.* KARL *and* INNKEEPER *enter.*)

KARL: What a good sleep I had! You have a fine inn here, and I would like to show my appreciation by giving you some more gold.

INNKEEPER: Oh, that won't be necessary. You have already given me enough, and besides, it is an honor to have such a rich gentleman staying at my inn.

KARL: How honest you are! Thank you. I must be on my way home now. (*Goes to* DONKEY)

INNKEEPER: Have a safe journey. (KARL *and* DONKEY *exit. Curtain.*)

*   *   *

SCENE 6

TIME: *The next day.*
SETTING: *The bare cottage, as in Scene 4.*
AT RISE: KARL *enters.*

KARL: Father! I've returned!

FATHER (*Entering*): Karl, my son! You're home at last! You look well and happy.

JOHANN (*Entering*): Brother! Welcome home.

FATHER: Have you brought anything home from your travels?

KARL (*Nonchalantly*): Nothing but a donkey.

FATHER (*Disappointed*): A donkey? A goat would have been more useful.

KARL: You won't think that when you see *this* donkey. He's magic.

FATHER: Oh, no! More magic again.

JOHANN: I hope your magic will last longer than mine did.

FATHER: What does the donkey do—give you food, too, I suppose?

KARL: Better than that, Father. Whenever I pull the donkey's ear and say, "Brickelbrit," gold coins pour from his mouth.

JOHANN (*In disbelief*): I don't believe it! Bring your donkey in!

KARL: Very well. (*Brings in* DONKEY) Now, watch. (*Pulls* DONKEY's *ear*) "Brickelbrit."

DONKEY: Hee-haw. (*Nothing happens.*)

FATHER: Where is the gold, Karl?

KARL: I don't know. Something must have gone wrong.

JOHANN: Your magic disappeared just as quickly as mine did!

FATHER: Don't worry. I am happy to have my two sons home. Now, if only your sister were here, too! But she has been gone for months now, seeking her fortune.

KARL: Yes, I hope that Anna is well. But I'm worried about her because she is frail and helpless.

JOHANN: Don't worry. Anna will be fine. She can take care of herself. (*Curtain*)

*　　*　　*

SCENE 7

SETTING: *The tapestry factory, with loom. Scene may be played in front of curtain.*

AT RISE: WEAVER *and* ANNA *are onstage, talking together.*

WEAVER: You have done a fine job here, Anna. You are the best weaver we have had for many years. I am sorry to see you leave.

ANNA: I am sorry to leave, too, but now that I have saved money, I must go home to my father.

WEAVER: It is dangerous to travel alone through these parts, Anna. Please take this to protect yourself. (*Hands* ANNA *a stick*) It is a token of my appreciation and affection for you.

ANNA: Thank you. (*Without enthusiasm*) That will be a great help.

WEAVER: This is not an ordinary stick, Anna, but a magic stick which will protect you against any danger.

ANNA (*Surprised*): A magic stick! How does it work?

WEAVER: If ever you are in danger, just say, "Stick, protect me," and the stick will begin to strike your attackers. It will not stop until you say, "Stick—stop."

ANNA (*Excited*): My, what a wonderful stick! How can I ever thank you? Now I shall be safe on my journey home. Goodbye—and thank you again.
WEAVER: Goodbye, Anna. Have a safe journey. (*Curtain*)

*   *   *

SCENE 8

TIME: *That evening.*
SETTING: *Same as Scene 3.*
AT RISE: ANNA *enters, holding her magic stick.* INNKEEPER *appears from the inn.*

ANNA: I have been walking for many hours. I must sit down for a while to rest.
INNKEEPER: Good evening, young lady. Why is a young girl like you traveling alone? Don't you know it isn't safe?
ANNA: Don't worry about me! I can take care of myself.
INNKEEPER: Yes, if you say so. But why don't you stay here and work at my inn?
ANNA: Thank you, sir, but I'm on my way home.
INNKEEPER: You'll change your mind when you hear how clever I am. Listen. Just this week I tricked two foolish lads who came by here on the way to their father's cottage in Sneiderdorf.
ANNA (*Aside*): Sneiderdorf! That's where I live.
INNKEEPER: One of them had a magic table, and the other, a magic donkey. I stole them and gave the two men a false table and donkey instead.
ANNA (*Aside*): They must have been my brothers.
INNKEEPER: So, you see, I am clever, and rich, too. Why not work here for a time?

ANNA: I'll have to think about it. Where are the magic table and donkey?

INNKEEPER: I am hiding them in my barn. I don't want anyone to know about them.

ANNA (*Coyly*): My! How clever of you!

INNKEEPER: Now, come inside, and I will give you something to eat.

ANNA: I really must be on my way, sir.

INNKEEPER (*Insisting*): Yes, yes, come in.

ANNA: No, I can't. I must go.

INNKEEPER (*Pulling* ANNA's *arm*): Just come in for one minute.

ANNA: Stop! Let me go! (*Calls*) "Stick, protect me." (*Stick hits* INNKEEPER *over and over.*)

INNKEEPER: Ouch, ooh, make it stop! Get it off me! Ow! Ooh! Stop! Stop!

ANNA: First you must promise me that you'll let me have the table and donkey. They belong to my brothers.

INNKEEPER (*Still being hit by stick*): I promise! I promise! Just make this stick stop!

ANNA: Then you must promise me that you'll never trick or cheat any other customers.

INNKEEPER: I promise! Only make the stick stop!

ANNA: Very well. "Stick—stop." (*Stick stops.*)

INNKEEPER (*In pain*): Oh, my poor head.

ANNA: That should teach you never to be dishonest again. Now come and help me put the table on the donkey's back. I must return home.

INNKEEPER: Yes, I'm coming. But please don't set that stick on me again. (*They exit. Curtain.*)

*   *   *

Scene 9

Time: *The next day.*
Setting: *The bare cottage again, as in Scene 4.*
At Rise: Anna *enters.*

Anna: Father! Father! It's Anna! I've come back!

Father (*Entering*): My child! How good to see you!

Karl (*Entering*): Anna, dear sister, you're home! I have been worried about you.

Johann (*Entering*): See, Karl! I was right. I told you we didn't have to worry about her.

Anna: It's wonderful to see you all again—and from now on, we will have no more worries. (*Brings on table and donkey*) Karl and Johann, I have returned with the real magic table and donkey. The thieving innkeeper stole these from you, and gave you false ones in their place.

Johann: So the Innkeeper is to blame!

Karl: He tricked us both. I can't believe it!

Father: The table and donkey are magic, after all. Karl and Johann, I should never have doubted you.

Anna: Father, many of our friends and neighbors have been kind and helpful to you while we were gone. Call them together and we shall eat and drink to our heart's content. I shall fill all their pockets with gold, too.

Father: What a splendid idea! It's so good to have my wonderful family with me again. (*Curtain*)

THE END

The Table, the Donkey and the Stick

PRODUCTION NOTES

Number of puppets: 8 hand or rod puppets or marionettes (the same Donkey can be used for each role).

Playing Time: 25 minutes.

Costumes: Typical German country dress, such as dirndls and *lederhosen*.

Properties: Cottage furniture, built in three separate units so that each can be removed as a section, as directed in Scene 1; carpenter's bench, with wood and tools on it; magic table, which has a second top hinged to the back edge, so that it can be flipped quickly to reveal "food" glued to this hidden top (use the same table for the second table); gold coins threaded together (placed inside head of Donkey and pulled out of Donkey's mouth as indicated); magic stick, which should be large and on a heavy, strong wire for good control.

Setting: Simplify all the scenery because of the nine scene changes. The cottage interior is the main back set. The inn can be a painted drop in front of the curtain. The carpenter's shop and the tapestry factory scenes can be done in front of the curtain. For the carpentry shop, use a workbench to suggest the set, and for the tapestry shop, a loom.

Lighting: Lower the lights and bring them up again, to indicate the passage of time, in the scenes at the inn.

Sound: No special effects. German folk dances may be played as background music, if desired.

ANANSI AND THE BOX OF STORIES

An early African legend

Characters

ANANSI, *the spider man*
NYAMI, *the sky god*
OSEBO, *the leopard of the terrible teeth*
MMBORO, *the hornets who sting like fire*
MOATIA, *the fairy whom no man sees*

BEFORE RISE: ANANSI *enters, addresses audience.*

ANANSI: How do you do? I am Anansi, the spider man. Do
you like a good story? In Africa, stories are called
"spider stories," for they are often about me. (*In sing-
song or chant; sound of drums is heard*) We do not really
mean, we do not really mean, that what we are about to
say is true. A story, a story; let it come, let it go, let it
begin . . . . (*A large web appears on one side of the stage.*)
Many years ago, oh, small children, there were no
stories on earth to hear. All the stories belonged to
Nyami, the sky god. He kept them in a golden box next
to his royal stool. I will go up to him on my spider web
and speak to him. (ANANSI *climbs the web, as curtains
open.*)

*   *   *

51

SCENE 1

SETTING: *The sky god's throne among the clouds.*

AT RISE: NYAMI *is sitting on his throne. Golden box is next to throne.* ANANSI *enters, bows.*

ANANSI: O great sky god, Nyami, I wish to speak to you.

NYAMI: Who are you, and what is it that you wish to talk to the great sky god about?

ANANSI: I am Anansi, the spider man, and I wish to buy your stories.

NYAMI: Oh, yes, Anansi—our little spinner of stories. (*Laughs*) You wish to buy my stories, do you?

ANANSI: Yes, great god.

NYAMI: Very well. The price of my stories is that you bring me Osebo, the leopard of the terrible teeth; Mmboro, the hornets who sting like fire; and Moatia, the fairy whom no man sees.

ANANSI: I shall gladly pay the price.

NYAMI (*Laughing*): How can a weak old man like you, so small, pay my price?

ANANSI: I shall return with what you ask, Nyami.

NYAMI (*Laughing again*): We shall see about that.

ANANSI: Goodbye for now, Nyami. (ANANSI *exits. Curtain*)

*   *   *

SCENE 2

SETTING: *The forest.*

AT RISE: OSEBO *slinks in and crosses stage. Drumbeat is heard.*

OSEBO: I'm hungry. What is there for Osebo, leopard of the terrible teeth, to eat? (ANANSI *enters, sees* OSEBO, *speaks aside to audience.*)

ANANSI: There is Osebo, the leopard that I must capture for Nyami. Let me see if I can trick him. (*Greets* OSEBO) Hello there, Osebo.

OSEBO (*Roaring*): Aha! Anansi—you are just in time to be my dinner.

ANANSI: As for that, what will happen will happen. But first let us play the binding binding game.

OSEBO: The binding binding game? How is it played?

ANANSI: With creepers from the vine. (*Takes rope from off-stage*) I will bind you by your foot and foot. Then I will untie you and you can tie me up.

OSEBO: Very well. Then I'll eat you. (ANANSI *ties up* OSEBO.)

ANANSI: Are you tied up tight?

OSEBO: Nice and tight! That's very good, Anansi. Now, untie me.

ANANSI: I will untie you later, Osebo. Now, are you ready to meet Nyami, the sky god?

OSEBO: Oh, no! Let me go! You tricked me! What a dunce I am!

ANANSI: I'll tie you to a tree and come for you later.

OSEBO: Oh, noooo! (ANANSI *pulls* OSEBO *offstage. Curtain*)

*   *   *

SCENE 3

SETTING: *A different part of the forest. There is a hornets' nest on a tree. Individual hornets on wires, and all connected at the base, are in nest.*

At Rise: Anansi *enters with a banana leaf on his head, and holding a calabash jug.*

Anansi: Now, let me see. I have a banana leaf to cover my head and a calabash jug to hold my guests. (*Buzzing of hornets is heard.*) And there is the nest of Mmboro, the hornets who sting like fire. Capturing Mmboro is the second task that Nyami wants me to accomplish. Now, this is what I will do: first, I must pour water over my head (*Pours from jug over his own head*), and then over the hornets' nest. (*He pours from jug over nest.* Mmboro *appear.* Anansi *calls to* Mmboro.) It's raining. It's raining. Mmboro, shouldn't you fly into my calabash so that the rain will not tatter your wings?

Mmboro (*With buzzing sound*): Thank you. Thank you, Anansi. (Mmboro *buzz and fly into calabash jug.* Anansi *plugs the jug.*)

Anansi: There! Now I've stopped up the calabash jug. Mmboro, you are ready to meet Nyami, the sky god. (*Loud buzzing is heard.*)

Mmboro (*From inside jug*): Let us out! (*They continue to buzz as* Anansi *exits with jug. Curtain*)

*   *   *

Scene 4

Setting: *Another part of the forest. Tree is left; bush, right.*
At Rise: Anansi *enters, carrying wooden doll and a bowl.*

Anansi: Here is my third trap, which I will use to capture Moatia, the fairy no man sees. I will set this wooden doll, holding a wooden bowl, by the flamboyant tree.

(*He puts doll down.*) This is where fairies like to dance. Now I'll cover the doll with sticky latex gum from the trees. (*He pours from bowl over the doll.*) That will make the wooden doll very sticky to the touch. I'll fill the bowl with pounded yams. (*Puts bowl in front of doll*) Now I'll hold the wooden doll by a string and hide behind that bush. I'll just wait for Moatia—let's see what happens. (*He hides.*)

MOATIA (*Entering*): What a beautiful day for dancing! No one is here. No one ever sees Moatia. (*She dances about, then sees doll and bowl; to doll*) Look here! Gum baby! Gum baby! I am hungry. May I eat some of your yams? (ANANSI *pulls the string and doll moves a bit.*) You nod your head. All right, I will eat. (*She eats from bowl.*) Hmmm. Delicious! Oh, I ate it all up. Thank you, gum baby. (*Pause*) Don't you reply when I thank you? You should say, "You're welcome." (*Pause*) Gum baby! I'll slap your crying place unless you answer me. (*Pause*) All right, then. (*She slaps doll. Her hand sticks to doll.*) Let go of my hand, or I'll slap you again. All right—there! (*She slaps doll with other hand, and it sticks.*) You let go. I'll get very angry. Let go, or I'll kick you. (*Pause*) All right, then! (*Kicks with left foot*) Oh! (*It sticks.*) Let go of my foot, gum baby! Let go, I say! I'll kick you again. (*She kicks with right foot and is stuck again.*) Oh, no! What will I do now? (*Cries*)

ANANSI (*Coming out*): Are you ready to meet the sky god, Moatia?

MOATIA: Anansi, it's you! You tricked me! Let me go right away! (*Struggles but cannot get free.*)

ANANSI (*Bringing* OSEBO *and jug onstage*): I have Osebo of the terrible teeth, and Mmboro, the hornets. I'll spin a web around all of you. (*Brings web from offstage, throws it over* MOATIA, OSEBO *and jug*) Now, off we go, up to the sky god. (*He takes them offstage and exits. Curtain*)

*   *   *

SCENE 5

SETTING: *Same as Scene 1.*

AT RISE: NYAMI *is sitting on throne.* OSEBO, *the jug containing* MMBORO, *and* MOATIA *are around the throne.* ANANSI *stands before throne.*

ANANSI: I have returned, O great sky god.

NYAMI: Why have you come back?

ANANSI: I am prepared to pay the price you asked for your golden box of stories. (*Gestures*) Osebo, the leopard of the terrible teeth.

OSEBO (*Growling*): Grrrr!

ANANSI: Mmboro, the hornets who sting like fire.

MMBORO (*Angrily*): Bzzzz!

ANANSI: And Moatia, the fairy whom no man sees.

MOATIA: Let me go. Let me go!

NYAMI: Little Anansi, the spider man, you have paid the price I asked for my stories. From this day, and forever, my stories belong to Anansi. They shall be called "spider stories."

ANANSI: Thank you, Nyami, O great sky god.

NYAMI: Here is my golden box of stories. (*Hands box to* ANANSI) Return to earth now. Open the box and release all the stories to make the world a happy, happy place.

ANANSI: Goodbye. (ANANSI *bows, takes golden box, and exits.*)

NYAMI: Goodbye, Anansi, the spider man. (*Curtain closes.*)

ANANSI (*Entering in front of curtain*): This is my story which I have told. If it be sweet, or if it be not sweet, take some elsewhere, and let some come back to me. (ANANSI *bows and exits. Curtain*)

THE END

Anansi and the Box of Stories

PRODUCTION NOTES

Number of Puppets: 5 hand or rod puppets, or marionettes.

Playing Time: 15 minutes.

Costumes: Anansi is a very old thin black man. He has gray hair and wears a loin cloth and animal skin over his chest. Nyami is large, and wears African robes and a turban. Osebo has spots and large teeth. Mmboro are individual hornets (or bees) on wires, all connected at the base. Moatia wears a simple tunic with wings.

Properties: Spider web made from rope; rope for Osebo; jug made from a gourd; banana leaf; wooden doll (stylized in the African manner); wooden bowl.

Setting: Scenes 1 and 5: the sky god's throne, a large, wicker, high-backed chair, is center. Clouds are seen in the sky behind throne. Scenes 2, 3 and 4: the forest. This could be a series of painted sections of forest, or trees hung in various arrangements for each scene.

Lighting: No special effects.

Sound: Native African music; drums; as indicated in text.

ALI BABA AND THE FORTY THIEVES

Adapted from The Arabian Nights

Characters

ALI BABA, *a woodcutter*
KASSIM, *his brother*
MORGANA, *Ali Baba's wife*
SHAHRIAR, *Kassim's wife*
MUSTAPHA, *robber chief*
ABDULLA, *Mustapha's helper*
NARRATOR

SCENE 1

SETTING: *Outdoor area in front of a cave. A large rock and tree are at one side.*
AT RISE: ALI BABA *enters.*

NARRATOR: This is the story of how Ali Baba and his wife Morgana outwitted forty dangerous thieves. It all began one day as Ali Baba was returning from selling his wood in the marketplace.
ALI BABA: Oh, I am exhausted! I've been up since dawn, and have sold all the firewood that I gathered. (*Looks at hand*) These pennies will not help Morgana and me very much. There isn't much you can buy with a few pennies nowadays. If only my family hadn't lost all its money and possessions to that terrible band of thieves. They have looted all the families of the countryside. Just what

will we do? (*Sound of band of thieves singing is heard from offstage.*) That must be the forty thieves now! I had better hide somewhere—but where? (*Looks up*) I know! Up in that tree. No. (*Looks at rock*) Better still, behind that rock. (*He hides.*)

MUSTAPHA (*Entering with* ABDULLA, *carrying bags*): Have the men camp over there, Abdulla. (*Points offstage*) You and I will enter the cave by ourselves.

ABDULLA: As you wish, Chief Mustapha. (*Calls offstage*) Comrades! Camp right where you are for a few minutes. Your chief and I will be joining you soon.

MUSTAPHA: Good. (*Facing cave*) Now, I'll say the magic words. (*Calls*) OPEN SESAME! (*Set piece covering mouth of cave moves aside, and precious jewels and gold are seen within cave.*)

ABDULLA: It always thrills me to see all this gold and these jewels. (*He puts the bag he carries inside cave.*) This is a perfect place to hide my—er—our treasure.

MUSTAPHA: Don't allow yourself to be tempted, Abdulla! If you ever decided to come to the cave by yourself, we would see to it that you would not get out again. You'd be a prisoner in the cave forever.

ABDULLA: Great chief, I had no such thoughts.

MUSTAPHA: You had better not! (*They finish placing bags inside cave.*) Come on, now. We must be on our way. We have more poor folk to rob before the sun sets.

ADBULLA (*Archly*): And a few to rob after the sun sets, as well.

MUSTAPHA: Of course! (*They both laugh.*) Now, stand aside. (*Calls*) CLOSE SESAME. (*Cave closes. They go offstage, laughing. Sound of thieves' song is heard again, as they exit.*)

ALI BABA (*Coming out cautiously*): Hm-m-m. Have they gone? Yes! The coast is clear. I heard the words they said to open the cave. Do I dare to try them? I think I

shall. (*Calls*) OPEN SESAME! (*Cave opens.*) Look! (*In awe*)
Caskets of jewels, bags of gold, costly rugs and tapestries
and bolts of silks. (*Shocked*) Wait! Look! Those clothes
and jewels belonged to my family. They were stolen
from us years ago. It would not be wrong to take what is
rightfully ours. (*He takes objects out of cave.*) There! Now
to close the cave. (*Calls*) CLOSE SESAME! (*The cave closes.*)
I'd better go home before the robbers return. Oh, what
luck I have had today! (*He exits. Curtain*)

*   *   *

SCENE 2

SETTING: *Interior of Ali Baba's humble house.*
AT RISE: MORGANA *is cleaning the house, talking to herself.*

MORGANA (*Worried*): Where can Ali Baba be? He is un-
usually late today. I hope nothing has happened to him.
ALI BABA (*Running in, carrying riches*): Oh, Morgana, good
wife, see what I have brought home. All the riches that
once were ours! We are no longer poor.
MORGANA (*Amazed*): Oh, my! Can it be? Do my eyes de-
ceive me? Let's see if it is all there. I have borrowed
Shahriar's measuring cup, and we can measure the gold
coins with that. (*Gets cup*)
ALI BABA: Good! Now, let's see. (*Measuring the coins*) Here
are some coins.
NARRATOR: Ali Baba and his wife carefully measured the
gold and counted their jewels to see if everything was
there. The next day, Morgana returned the measuring
cup to her sister-in-law, Shahriar. (*Curtain*)

*   *   *

SCENE 3

SETTING: *Room in the well-appointed house of Kassim and Shahriar. Rugs and tapestries are draped about.*
AT RISE: *Sound of a knock is heard.* SHAHRIAR *enters and crosses the stage.*

SHAHRIAR (*Calling*): Yes, yes! I'm coming. (*Crossly*) Who could that be? It's very early for a caller. Come in. Come in!

MORGANA (*Entering, with measuring cup*): Good afternoon, Shahriar, dear sister-in-law.

SHAHRIAR: What do you mean afternoon? Is it that late already? What do you want anyway?

MORGANA: I've only come to return your measuring cup. (*Hands cup to* SHAHRIAR) Thank you very much.

SHAHRIAR (*Angrily*): Well, it's about time you brought it back! (*Stops*) Hm-m-m. (*Distracted; turns away from* MORGANA) You can go now.

MORGANA: Thank you again.

SHAHRIAR: Yes, yes. Be off now. (MORGANA *exits.*) Hm-m-m. (*Calls*) Kassim. Kassim, my husband, come out here!

KASSIM (*From offstage*): What is it?

SHAHRIAR: I have something important to show you. Come here. (*She holds up a large gold coin.*)

KASSIM (*Entering*): What is it? (*Sees coin*) Where did you get that? It's pure gold!

SHAHRIAR: From your brother's wife, Morgana. It was stuck in the bottom of the measuring cup she had borrowed from me. (*Sarcastically*) Your brother, the woodcutter, is so poor that he borrows a cup to measure his gold coins, eh?

KASSIM: Hm-m-m. I'm going to have to find out where he got that. Give it to me. (*Tries to take coin*)

SHAHRIAR (*Moving away*): No! I found it, so it's mine.

KASSIM: Keep it, then. I'll find others. (*He runs out.*)

NARRATOR: And so Kassim rushed to Ali Baba's house and forced Ali Baba to tell him where he got the gold. Then he rushed to the cave. (*Curtain*)

* * *

SCENE 4

SETTING: *Same as Scene 1.*

AT RISE: KASSIM *rushes in.*

KASSIM (*Facing cave*): Now, what is that word? (*Alarmed*) Oh, no! Did I forget the right words? Let's see. OPEN BARLEY! No, that's not it. (*Pauses*) Hm-m-m. OPEN WHEAT! No, that's not it, either. I remember. (*Calls*) OPEN SESAME! (*Cave swings open, revealing* MUSTAPHA *and* ABDULLA *inside cave.* KASSIM *cries out in fright.*)

MUSTAPHA (*Slyly*): So—you want to be in the cave of riches, do you? Assist him, Abdulla. (ABDULLA *rushes to capture* KASSIM *and pulls him inside cave.* MUSTAPHA *and* ABDULLA *leave cave.*) Now, stay there forever, thief! (*Calls*) CLOSE SESAME!

KASSIM (*As cave closes*): Ohhhhhhhh!

MUSTAPHA: Now, let that be a lesson to anyone who tries to steal thieves' gold! (*He and* ABDULLA *rush out. Lights may dim briefly to indicate passage of time.*)

NARRATOR: Poor Kassim was forced to be a prisoner in the cave he had wanted to see. Shahriar became worried when he didn't come home and went to Ali Baba to tell him that Kassim was missing. Ali Baba thought his brother might be trapped in the cave, and so he returned there to check.

ALI BABA (*Entering*): Kassim must be here! I don't see any of the thieves, so I'll use the magic words to open the cave. (*Calls*) OPEN SESAME! (*Cave opens and* KASSIM *falls out into his arms.*)

KASSIM: Oh, thank you, dear brother, Ali Baba, for saving me!

ALI BABA: Quickly, Kassim! We must leave this place before any of the thieves return.

KASSIM: Yes, by all means! (*Greedily*) Just let me take a few jewels, first.

ALI BABA: No! The treasure is cursed. Don't touch any of it. We must be off. (*They race out.*)

ABDULLA (*Entering*): So! I was wise to keep guard over the cave. Now I will follow them and see where they live. (*Laughs*) Ha, ha! (*He exits quickly. Curtain*)

*   *   *

SCENE 5

SETTING: *Street scene in front of Ali Baba's house. Three or four houses are in a row. Ali Baba's house, at center, has a working door.*

AT RISE: ALI BABA *and* KASSIM *enter.*

NARRATOR: Ali Baba and Kassim arrived soon at Ali Baba's house, unaware that Abdulla had followed them.

ALI BABA (*Calling*): Wife! Morgana! We're home. (MORGANA *and* SHAHRIAR *come out.*) Kassim is safe!

SHAHRIAR (*Rushing to* KASSIM *and hugging him*): Oh, Kassim!

You are here at last. My poor husband, what did the thieves do to you?

KASSIM (*Wearily*): Let us go home, so I can rest, Shahriar. I'll tell you all about it there. (*They exit.*)

ALĪ BABA: We should go in, too, Morgana. I must tell you, also, about this adventure.

MORGANA: Right away, husband. Go in. I will join you in a minute. (*He enters the house and she goes to one side and hides behind tree.*)

ABDULLA (*Entering*): Aha. That house is where they live. Heh, heh! They can't fool Abdulla. I'll mark their front door with a large "X" and then bring Mustapha to see where the culprit lives. (*He puts a large "X" on* ALI BABA's *door, then exits.*)

MORGANA (*Coming out of hiding*): Just as I thought! Ali Baba and Kassim were followed. (*Pauses*) I know! I'll mark these other doors, too. The thieves will never know which door is the right one. (*She marks other doors onstage with an "X."*) There! Perfect. (*She enters her house and closes door behind her as* MUSTAPHA *and* ABDULLA *enter.*)

MUSTAPHA: Now, show me, Abdulla. Which door is theirs?

ABDULLA: I marked it. (*Points to a door*) It's this one. No! (*Turns to another*) This one.

MUSTAPHA: You fool! The peasants were smarter than you. They marked all the doors!

ABDULLA: Now we'll never know where the rascal lives who stole our treasure.

MUSTAPHA: I'm not so sure about that. Look! (*Points to floor*) A gold coin was dropped on the doorstep of that house. It must have been from our hoard. (*Laughs*) We found the right house after all!

ABDULLA: What luck we have!

MUSTAPHA: It is not luck, but good powers of observation.

Go now, and bring back all forty of our thieves. There are forty empty oil jars on the dock next to this house— tell the men to hide there. And, have an extra jar filled with oil, too. Now, hurry!

ABDULLA (*Excited*): Yes, yes, right away! We'll teach those peasants a lesson. (*Laughs*) Heh, heh, heh! (*Exits*)

MUSTAPHA: Now, to do my dirty work. (*He knocks on* ALI BABA's *door, and* ALI BABA *opens it*.) Good afternoon.

ALI BABA: Good afternoon, good merchant. How can I help you?

MUSTAPHA: Kind gentleman, I need a place to sleep tonight. I will pay you well if you let me stay here. I have forty jars of olive oil on the dock nearby.

ALI BABA: Why, certainly, you may stay here. I cannot refuse such a generous offer. (*Calls*) Morgana! Arrange a bed for this generous merchant. Tonight we will have a guest in our house. (*To* MUSTAPHA) Come in. Come in! (*They enter house. Curtain*)

* * *

SCENE 6

SETTING: *The dock. Part of Ali Baba's house and river are at rear. Several oil jars are onstage.*

AT RISE: MORGANA *enters.*

NARRATOR: Ali Baba did not recognize the merchant as Mustapha, the thief, and opened his house to him. But, Morgana was suspicious, and cautious as well. She went to the back of their house, which was on a dock overlooking a rushing river, and there she found forty large oil jars.

MORGANA: Look at all these oil containers! I wonder if they really contain oil. I will knock on one of them. (*She knocks on jar.*)

VOICE OF ABDULLA (*As if inside jar*): Yes, we're here, Master. Everything is ready for the attack. Is it time now for all forty of us to come out?

MORGANA (*Aside*): What is this? I must disguise my voice! (*In deep voice*) No, not yet. I will let you know.

VOICE OF ABDULLA: Good, Chief. We will wait for your signal.

MORGANA (*Aside*): These jars must be hiding the forty thieves that Ali Baba told me about. What will I do to save us? (*Pauses*) I know! I will seal the top of each jar, and then tip all of them into the river. (*She pushes jars backwards into river.*) By the time the thieves can get out of these, they'll be miles away from here—maybe even in the ocean.

NARRATOR: And so Morgana sealed each and every one of the jars, and pushed them into the rushing river. And for all we know, the thieves may still be sailing the high seas. (*Curtain*)

*   *   *

SCENE 7

SETTING: *Same as Scene 2.*

AT RISE: ALI BABA *and* MUSTAPHA *sit at a table, laughing and drinking.*

NARRATOR: Meanwhile, Ali Baba was entertaining Mustapha, the false merchant, in his home.

MUSTAPHA (*Laughing*): What a good table you set, Ali Baba! You must have inherited quite a fortune.

ALI BABA: I have only what truly belongs to me, kind merchant. I have been fortunate.

MUSTAPHA: I see. Such fortune can always be helped along. I will see what I can do.

ALI BABA: Why, that is kind of you. (MORGANA *enters with jar. She places jar at one side of stage.*) Here is my wife. She has come to dance for you.

MORGANA: For your pleasure, sir merchant. (*Music is played offstage, as she dances.*)

MUSTAPHA: Ahhh! So graceful! You are lucky to have such a wife, sir.

MORGANA (*Going to jar and picking it up*): This is called the olive oil dance. (*Dancing with jar*) Just pick up the jar, move about (*Turning jar upside down and placing it over* MUSTAPHA's *head*), then turn the jar upside down.

MUSTAPHA (*Struggling to get jar off; stunned*): What! Ugh! Ughhh! (*He falls over onto ground, unable to get jar off.*)

ALI BABA (*Shocked*): What are you doing, Morgana?

MORGANA: This man is not a merchant at all, husband, but the robber chief, Mustapha. Look! (*Points to* MUSTAPHA's *belt*) In his belt!

ALI BABA: A dagger! He meant to kill me.

MORGANA: And his men were hidden outside! They meant to kill us all, but they are already on their way again, now. They've decided to become sailors instead of thieves. (*She laughs.*)

ALI BABA: Sailors?

MORGANA: Yes! They are in their oil-jar boats, sailing away down to the sea.

ALI BABA: Morgana, you've outwitted Mustapha and his thieves—and saved our lives, too.

KASSIM (*Entering*): What has happened? Why is this man on the floor with a jar on his head?

ALI BABA: He is learning not to be greedy. And let that be a lesson to you as well, Kassim. My clever wife Morgana has saved us all!

KASSIM: Hurray for Morgana!

MORGANA: And so goes another one of the thousand and one Arabian nights. (*To audience*) Good night! (*She closes curtain.*)

THE END

Ali Baba and the Forty Thieves

PRODUCTION NOTES

Number of Puppets: 6 hand or rod puppets or marionettes.

Playing Time: 25 minutes.

Costumes: Traditional Arab dress, such as, full trousers or "harem pants" for men and women; veils for women; turbans for men. Use a fairy-tale book with good illustrations to get ideas for costumes. Mustapha must have a dagger in his belt.

Properties: Bags of gold for thieves and Ali Baba to carry; measuring cup on a wire for easy handling; gold piece (sewn or glued into Shahriar's hand); a number of large ceramic jars (should be flat on one side to lie on stage floor when Morgana pushes them); a large, full-dimensional jar on a wire for Scene 7.

Setting: An outside area, near a cave; interior of a humble house; richly-appointed house interior; street of houses; dock on a river. Sets should be simple, because five are needed; model them after illustrations in books, to create an Arabian flavor. In Scene 1, the cave front can be separate from the main set, or on hinges, and either moved to one side or opened, as indicated in text. In Scene 5, Ali Baba's house is center stage, and has a working door. Use a piece of chalk and mark X's on the doors, as indicated, or else "flip-over" squares on the doors with an X drawn on one side and released when the puppet "draws" the X.

Lighting: No special effects. The dock scene can be done in blue.

Sound: Live or recorded music for thieves' song, and dance, as indicated in text. "Scheherazade," or Arabian-sounding music, would be appropriate.

PEREZ AND MARTINA

A traditional Mexican story

Characters

MARTINA, *a cockroach*
ROOSTER, *Señor Gallo*
PIG, *Señor Cerdo*
CAT, *Señor Gato*
PEREZ, *a mouse*
DOCTOR OWL
JUSTICE OF THE PEACE, *a Chihuahua*
DANCING COUPLES, *cockroaches and mice*
NARRATOR

SCENE 1

SETTING: *The area outside Martina's house. The front of the house is seen, including a door and window.*
AT RISE: MARTINA *is sweeping and singing to herself.*

NARRATOR: Once upon a time, in Mexico, a lovely cock-roach named Martina lived in a pretty house all by her-self.
MARTINA (*Stopping sweeping*): Oh! What's this? A coin! I almost swept it away. I think I will spend it. Hm-m-m. What can I buy? I know! I will buy rouge for my cheeks—bright, red rouge—to make myself look pretty! I'll sit on my porch and wait for a gentleman to come courting. (*Hums again as she exits*)

NARRATOR: And so Martina went to the store and bought the rouge, bright and red. She carefully put it on her face and she looked very pretty. She came out of her house and sat on her porch and waited.

MARTINA (*Re-entering from house*): What a perfect day! (*Holds up a mirror*) I look so pretty. I do wish someone would come along.

ROOSTER (*Offstage*): Cock-a-doo-dle-doo! Cock-a-doo-dle-doo!

MARTINA: What is that noise? Who is it?

ROOSTER (*Entering*): Fair Martina, it is I, the proud and handsome rooster, Señor Gallo. I have come to ask for your hand. Would you like to marry handsome me? Cock-a-doo-dle-doo!

MARTINA: Be on your way, Señor Gallo.

ROOSTER: But I am just the right one for you.

MARTINA: I will not marry a loud stuffed shirt like you. (*He exits.*)

PIG (*Entering*): Oink! Oink! Ah, little Martina, my dear.

MARTINA: What is it, Señor Cerdo?

PIG: I want you to marry me. I am very wealthy. Do you want to be my bride and live in my pigsty?

MARTINA: Señor Cerdo, how will you prove that you love me?

PIG: Oink—oink—oink! You will have the privilege of keeping house for me. You may wash my dishes, clean the floors and windows, sew my clothes, and do all the other chores.

MARTINA: I can do that at home for myself. Besides, your "oink-oinking" bothers me. Move on, piggy!

PIG: But I can give you anything you wish!

MARTINA: Go away.

PIG: Very well, but you'll be sorry. (*He exits, oinking.*)

MARTINA: What a pig! He was so dirty. I certainly do not want to marry him and live in a pigsty. (*She goes into her house.*)

CAT (*Entering*): Meow! Meow! Miss Martina, come out. (MARTINA *sticks her head out of window. In sly, oily tone*) Ah, Miss Martina, I understand you are looking for a husband. Do you want to marry me?

MARTINA: I don't trust you, Señor Gato. You have feline eating habits, and I fear I may lose my head or my friends if I become your wife. Please, go away.

CAT: Ridiculous! We would make a delightful couple. We could share mice together. Meow! I can sing, too. Listen. (*Meows*)

MARTINA: You've gone too far. Go away! (*She pulls her head back out of window.*)

CAT: Come back! Come back! (*Menacingly*) You'll be sorry, Martina. No one ever says no to Señor Gato. (*He exits.*)

NARRATOR: Poor Martina was frightened as can be. She hid in her little house until she knew the Cat had gone. About that time Perez, the mouse, appeared.

PEREZ (*Entering*): Squeak! Squeak! Miss Martina! Yoo-hoo! Where are you? Please come out. It is Perez, the mouse. Squeak! Squeak!

MARTINA (*Coming out of her house*): Oh, it is you, Perez.

PEREZ: Yes, beautiful Martina. Won't you marry Perez? I love you with all my mouse heart. I'll share my life with you forever. Be mine.

MARTINA: Will all be equally shared? The food, the work and the joy?

PEREZ: Of course, sweet Martina.

MARTINA: Then I shall marry you.

PEREZ: We will be so happy together.

MARTINA: Together, forever—Martina and Perez.

PEREZ: Martina and Perez. (*They exit into house.* CAT *appears.*)

CAT (*Laughing evilly*): Martina, Perez, and Señor Gato . . . And I will be the villain—and catch them both! (*He laughs, meows, and exits. Curtain*)

*   *   *

SCENE 2

SETTING: *Inside Martina's house. There is a large cooking pot, center stage. There may be other cooking utensils, and a window, if desired.*

AT RISE: PEREZ *is trimming the house with garlands of flowers. He finishes and falls asleep during* NARRATOR's *speech.*

NARRATOR: Perez and Martina arranged for the big day when they would get married. Perez helped Martina and trimmed the house for their first day together. (PEREZ *sits and goes to sleep.* MARTINA *enters. She is humming a tune and dusting. Sound of clock striking eight is heard.*)

MARTINA: Perez! Perez! (*She wakes him.*) Would you watch the beans while I go shopping? I must get a few more things for the wedding. It won't be long until we are husband and wife.

PEREZ: Si, si! The beans look good.

MARTINA: I am going to buy some other tasty food, too. Goodbye for now. I'll be back soon. Don't forget to look after the beans.

PEREZ: I won't forget. (*She exits.* PEREZ *looks into pot.*) Those beans look good! I'm so hungry after trimming the house that I think I'll just have one little taste. (*He takes taste.*) Those beans are delicious. I'll have another taste.

(*Tastes again*) Yum, yum. (*Puts head into pot*) Just . . . one more . . . bite. (*He falls in.*) Help! Help! I've fallen into the bean pot. HELP! (*He disappears.*)

MARTINA (*Entering with full basket; calling*): Perez! (*She sets basket down.*) Perez! Now, where could he be? I hope he hasn't run away. (*Sniffs the air*) Oh, no. Something's burning! The beans! (*She runs to pot, looks in.*) What's this in the pot? Oh, no! It is Perez. No, no! Help, help! Someone, help! Save my Perez. (*She cries.*)

ROOSTER (*Running in*): What's wrong, Martina?

MARTINA: Oh, Señor Gallo. My Perez fell into the bean pot. Please help me save him.

ROOSTER: Perez fell into the pot, did he? Here. Let's pull him out. (*Both reach into pot.*)

MARTINA *and* ROOSTER (*Together*): One, two, three! (PEREZ *is pulled out, but he does not move.*)

MARTINA: Perez! Oh, dear—oh, dear. Is he dead, Señor Gallo?

ROOSTER: No, just full of beans. I'll get the doctor. (*He exits.*)

PEREZ (*Groggily*): Martina—Martina. I stirred your beans. (*He moans.*)

MARTINA: Just stay still. The doctor is coming. My poor Perez!

DOCTOR (*Entering*): Ah, Martina. How is Perez? Let me see him. (DOCTOR *looks* PEREZ *over.*) Hm-m-m. Quick! Bring me my medicine bag.

MARTINA: Right away, Doctor Owl. (*She exits.*)

DOCTOR: Hm-m-m. He seems to be covered with beans.

MARTINA (*Returning with bag*): He has beans inside, too.

DOCTOR (*Looking into bag and naming each item that he takes out*): Hm-m-m. I need my saw, and my pills, my needle and thread, and a tortilla.

MARTINA: What is the tortilla for, Doctor?

DOCTOR: It is my lunch! Maybe I'll eat it now.

MARTINA: Please, Doctor. Just look after Perez!

DOCTOR: Oh, yes. Of course. Hm-mm. (*Takes mallet out of bag and hits* PEREZ *on head*)

PEREZ: Owww! That didn't feel good.

DOCTOR: It was necessary. Don't be such a baby, Perez.

MARTINA: Save him, Doctor. Save my Perez.

DOCTOR: Maybe he needs artificial respiration. (*He jumps up and down on* PEREZ.)

PEREZ: Get off me, Doctor Owl. I'm all right now.

MARTINA: My little mouse. You're alive!

PEREZ: Yes, dear Martina, I'm safe, thanks to you, Señor Gallo and Doctor Owl. I will clean myself up for the wedding. (*He exits.*)

MARTINA: Thank you, Doctor Owl. You have saved my Perez's life.

DOCTOR: You are welcome, Martina. My fee is three hundred pesos.

MARTINA: Three hundred pesos! Ohh! (*She faints.*)

DOCTOR (*Upset*): Someone help me. She has fainted. What do I do? Oh, dear.

CAT (*Entering*): Good afternoon, Doctor Owl. What's the matter here? Can I help?

OWL (*Frightened*): Good grief! It's the cat!

CAT: Say, Doctor Owl, what do you say we feast together on Perez Mouse and Martina?

DOCTOR: Help! Help! (*He runs off.*)

CAT: Now I'll catch Perez Mouse. I'll just hide over here and surprise him. (MARTINA *wakes up, sees* CAT.)

MARTINA: The Cat! I'll fix him. (*Turns bean pot over* CAT's *head*)

CAT: Ow-w-w-w! Help! I'm stuck in the bean pot! Hel-l-lp! (*He runs off.*)

MARTINA: Good! That takes care of that pesky Cat. (*Calls*) Perez! Come! Time to go to church! (PEREZ *enters.*)

PEREZ: Where is the bean pot?

MARTINA: I used it to teach the Cat a lesson. We'll not be bothered with him again!

PEREZ: My brave little Martina. (*They exit, laughing. Curtain*)

*　　*　　*

SCENE 3

SETTING: *The churchyard, decorated with flowers.*

AT RISE: *Mexican music is heard from offstage.* MARTINA, *in wedding dress and veil, enters with* PEREZ. JUSTICE OF THE PEACE *enters.*

NARRATOR: And so the big day came for Martina and Perez to be married. But the cat had his plans, as well. Poor Martina . . . poor Perez.

JUSTICE OF THE PEACE: Do you, Perez Mouse, take Martina for your wife?

PEREZ: I do, I do.

JUSTICE OF THE PEACE: And do you, Martina cockroach, take Perez for your husband?

MARTINA: I do, I do.

JUSTICE OF THE PEACE: Then I pronounce you husband and wife.

OFFSTAGE VOICES (*Cheering*): Hooray!

MARTINA: I have brought a piñata and now I will hang it up. (*Piñata appears. She pretends to pull it up by string, until it is over stage.*) It is heavy with candy and goodies. Don't let it fall on any of you. It might knock you out.

JUSTICE OF THE PEACE: We'll be careful. Now, let the celebration begin. (*Mexican dance music is heard.* DANCING COUPLES, *mice and cockroaches, appear and begin to dance.*) Here's to the happy couple.

PEREZ: Here's to my new wife!

CAT (*Appearing*): And here is to my next meal . . . Perez Mouse!

JUSTICE OF THE PEACE: Look out! It's the Cat! (CAT *chases* PEREZ *around stage.*)

MARTINA: And here's to my husband! (*She releases the piñata, which falls on* CAT's *head.*)

CAT: Owww! (*Faints*)

OFFSTAGE VOICES: Hooray! Long live Martina! Long live Perez! Long live the happy couple! (*Dancing and rejoicing continue as curtain closes.*)

THE END

Perez and Martina

PRODUCTION NOTES

Number of Puppets: 7 hand or rod puppets, or marionettes, for main characters, and 4 or more rod puppets for dancing couples.

Playing Time: 20 minutes.

Costumes: Mexican peasant clothes. Have Martina in two or three different costumes, if desired—one for the opening lines, another with her face made up as indicated in Scene 1, and another in a wedding dress and veil.

Properties: Broom; hand mirror; large cooking pot; wooden spoon; garlands of flowers; feather duster; shopping basket; doctor's bag, containing saw, pills, needle and thread, tortilla, and mallet; piñata, which must be on a thread so it can be pulled up to a screw eye at the top of the stage.

Setting: Scene 1, outside Martina's house: the front of the house is seen, including a door and window. Scene 2, inside Martina's house. Large cooking pot with wooden spoon is center stage. There is a window. Other cooking utensils may hang on wall. Scene 3, the churchyard, decorated with Mexican flowers. On backdrop is a simple church building with a spire or bell tower.

Lighting: No special effects.

Sound: Clock striking eight, as indicated in text. Mexican music for bridge between the scenes and also for the dances.

THE LEGEND OF URASHIMA

A Japanese folk tale

Characters

URASHIMA, *a young fisherman*
DAIGIN, *a boy*
TURTLE
DRAGON, *king of the sea*
EIGHT ARMS, *an octopus servant*
DANCING FISH
URASHIMA, *as an old man*
DAIGIN, *as an old man*
NARRATOR

SCENE 1

SETTING: *On the shore, near a little town in Japan. A boat is at center; hut is at right.*
AT RISE: URASHIMA *is preparing his boat for fishing.* DAIGIN *enters, with a walking stick.*

NARRATOR: This is the strange story of Urashima, a kind fisherman who lived in Japan. He cared for his parents, who lived with him in a little house near the sea. One day, while he was preparing to go fishing . . .
DAIGIN: What are you doing, Urashima?
URASHIMA: Oh, hello, Daigin. I am getting ready to fish.
DAIGIN: Are you going out to sea on a day like this? The clouds are gathering. It might rain.

URASHIMA: But, I must go, for I need to bring home money for my parents. They are too old to work.

DAIGIN: I'm not going to help my parents. I am going to run away.

URASHIMA: Don't do that, or your parents will worry about you. Wait here for me — I must get my lunch. I will be right back. (*He exits.*)

DAIGIN: Urashima is a fool. (TURTLE *appears.*) Hi! Look at the big turtle. (*Laughs*) What are you doing here, Turtle? (*Pauses*) So, you won't talk to me, huh? I'll teach you a lesson. (*He hits* TURTLE.) Take that, you dumb thing. (*Hits* TURTLE *again*) And that and that! (*Hits* TURTLE *again*)

URASHIMA (*Re-entering with lunch box*): Stop that, Daigin! Stop hitting that turtle!

DAIGIN: It's my turtle. I found it. I'll beat it if I want to. (*He hits* TURTLE *again.*)

URASHIMA: Stop! I'll give you my lunch in exchange for the turtle.

DAIGIN: What's in it?

URASHIMA: Roast pork, bean sprouts and rice cakes — your favorite.

DAIGIN: Hmmm. Very well. Give it to me. You can have the turtle. (DAIGIN *takes the lunch box and exits.*)

URASHIMA: Poor turtle! Here . . . (*Helps* TURTLE *to walk*) Swim out to sea, so that the cool water will soothe your back. And don't let anyone beat you again. (TURTLE *swims away and exits.*) Goodbye, friend Turtle. And now I must go out to sea. I hope the weather improves. It does look as if a storm is coming. (*He gets into boat, and it "floats" away. Curtain*)

*   *   *

Scene 2

SETTING: *At sea. Sky backdrop, and waves across stage.*
AT RISE: *Sound of wind howling is heard from offstage. The boat with* URASHIMA *in it is tossed about as if by waves.*

NARRATOR: Soon after Urashima set sail, a terrible storm did come up. Poor Urashima's life was in terrible danger.

URASHIMA: I had better try to bail. The water in the boat is getting very high! (*He bails.*) What will I do? I'll never get back to shore in this terrible storm. (*Frightened*) Ohhh!

TURTLE (*Calling from offstage*): Master Urashima. Master Urashima.

URASHIMA: Who is calling me? It must have been the wind. Or else I'm dreaming.

TURTLE (*Appearing*): Master Urashima. You aren't dreaming. It's your friend, the turtle. Don't you recognize me? I am the turtle you rescued from that bad boy.

URASHIMA: Yes, of course. My boat is about to sink. Can you help me?

TURTLE: Climb on my back and I will take you to the bottom of the ocean for a visit to the powerful dragon Kouramotchi. He is king of the oceans.

URASHIMA: But I will drown!

TURTLE: My magical powers will keep you safe—trust me.

URASHIMA: Very well. (URASHIMA *climbs onto* TURTLE. *They exit. The boat sinks. Curtain*)

*   *   *

SCENE 3

SETTING: *The Dragon's palace. A beautiful throne is center stage, and walls are covered with gem-like stones and corals.*
AT RISE: *Fish swim across the stage.* URASHIMA *and* TURTLE *enter.*

NARRATOR: Down, down, down they went until they came to the bottom of the ocean. They passed beautiful gardens no human eye had ever seen before. Finally, they arrived in front of a magnificent palace covered with pearls, lapis lazuli, agate and coral. The great door of the palace opened mysteriously before them.

URASHIMA: I have never seen anything quite so beautiful before.

TURTLE: You are a welcome guest, Master Urashima. It is time for Kouramotchi, the dragon king of the oceans, to arrive. Do not be frightened. He is most benevolent and generous. (*Sound of a gong is heard and* DRAGON *enters.*)

DRAGON: Welcome, Urashima. We respect you and wish you no harm. Because you saved the turtle, we wish to thank you, and hope that you will be our guest here in the palace. Everything is at your disposal. Your every wish shall be our command, and you may stay as long as you like. (*Sound of gong is heard again and* DANCING FISH *appear. Music is heard. They dance, then exit.*)

URASHIMA: How wonderful! Dancing fish. (*He applauds.*)

TURTLE: Every day you will be entertained by strange and wonderful events.

DRAGON: Eight Arms, the octopus, will take care of your every need. (EIGHT ARMS *enters. Each of his tentacles holds a different implement—toothbrush, comb, hairbrush, washcloth, a glass, a plate, chopsticks and a bottle.*)

EIGHT ARMS: Welcome, Urashima. I will show you to your quarters.

DRAGON: Each morning, an exciting new day under the sea will begin. This is now your new home.

URASHIMA: How splendid!

EIGHT ARMS: Come with me, now. (*They exit. Curtain*)

*   *   *

SCENE 4

TIME: *Several years later.*
SETTING: *Same as Scene 3.*
AT RISE: *Stage is empty.*

NARRATOR: And so Urashima began his life under the sea. He was happy there for many, many years. But eventually, the most beautiful things lose their charm. (URASHIMA *enters. Sound of a gong is heard.* DRAGON *enters.*)

DRAGON: Urashima, good friend, we hope that you have enjoyed your years with us.

URASHIMA: You all have been very kind to me, and have given me much pleasure. Now I wish to return to my parents' home, for I fear that they may have grown lonesome for me. Powerful King, please ask Turtle to take me back.

DRAGON: I have grown fond of you, and I will be sad to see you go. But I will grant your wish, Urashima. (*Sound of a gong is heard and* TURTLE *enters.*)

TURTLE: Yes, O Great King?

DRAGON: Our friend Urashima wishes to return home. Put him on your back and take him there.

TURTLE: As you command.

DRAGON: Urashima! (*Gets small box and puts it onstage*) Take this box as a reminder of me and the time you have spent with us under the sea. But heed this warning: never open the box. And so, farewell, Urashima. (DRAGON *disappears.*)

TURTLE: Come. Take the box. We must go before the tides turn once again.

URASHIMA (*Taking box*): Yes, let us go.

TURTLE: Get onto my back. (URASHIMA *climbs onto* TURTLE's *back.*) Off we go! (*They swim off. Curtain*)

*   *   *

SCENE 5

SETTING: *Same as Scene 1, except that hut appears abandoned.*

AT RISE: URASHIMA *enters, riding on* TURTLE. *He wears box on back.*

URASHIMA (*Getting down*): Goodbye, good friend. Thank you for bringing me home again. I shall never forget you.

TURTLE: Nor will I forget you, Urashima. Remember your good times under the sea! We shall all miss you.

URASHIMA: Goodbye!

TURTLE: Goodbye. (TURTLE *exits.*)

URASHIMA (*Turning to house; calling*): Mother! Father! (*Pauses*) Hmmm. They don't seem to answer. The house looks so old. What could have happened to it? (DAIGIN, *as an old man, enters.*) Here comes an old man. Perhaps he can tell me where my parents are. (*Stops* DAIGIN) Old man! Tell me — where is the old couple that lives in this house?

DAIGIN: That house has been deserted for many, many years. The people who lived in it died long ago. Their son, a fisherman called Urashima, was lost at sea and never heard from again.

URASHIMA (*Upset*): What are you saying? When was this?

DAIGIN: At least fifty years ago.

URASHIMA (*Shocked*): Alas! Fifty years! Not to see my parents — how sad! Time must be different under the sea. But, who are you?

DAIGIN: My name is Daigin.

URASHIMA (*Surprised*): Daigin! Don't you recognize me, Daigin? I am Urashima. I did not drown. I have lived under the sea with the fish all these years.

DAIGIN (*Overwhelmed*): Can it be? I don't understand. Tell me, how is it possible?

URASHIMA: I went down into the sea on the back of a turtle. The sea world is so beautiful that I stayed for a long time.

DAIGIN (*Still shocked*): I cannot believe it! You look as young as a boy. I see you carry a box on your back, Urashima. Does it hold some treasure from the sea?

URASHIMA: I don't know. (*Takes box from his back*) The Dragon King of the ocean gave it to me.

DAIGIN (*Excitedly*): Open it! Open it! It might be something wonderful.

URASHIMA: But, I cannot! The Dragon King warned me not to.

DAIGIN: Urashima, what does it matter now? You are no longer living under the sea.

URASHIMA (*Slowly*): Yes, I suppose you're right, Daigin. (*Firmly*) Yes, I will open the box. What does my homecoming matter now, with my parents gone? (*He opens box and white smoke comes out of it. There is a magical change and* URASHIMA *turns into an old man.*)

DAIGIN: Look! Look! Look at yourself. You have become an old man, just like me.

URASHIMA (*In a quivering voice*): You're right! The box must have held my youth. I'd been given eternal youth by the Dragon King, but now it has escaped. The enchantment has ended. (*Slowly*) Let us open this old house again, and live here until the end of our days. (URASHIMA *helps* DAIGIN *to go toward house.*) Come, Daigin. (*They enter house, as curtains close.*)

THE END

The Legend of Urashima

Production Notes

Number of Puppets: 7 hand or rod puppets, or marionettes; as many puppets as desired for Dancing Fish.

Playing Time: 20 minutes.

Costumes: Urashima and Daigin wear loose shirts and trousers. Urashima may also wear straw coolie hat and straw raincoat cape. Eight Arms has one of the following attached to each tentacle — toothbrush, comb, hairbrush, washcloth, a glass, a plate, chopsticks, and a bottle. Urashima and Daigin as old men wear tattered clothes, and have gray hair. One may also have a long gray beard. Dancing Fish may be individual puppets, or else on mobile controls.

Properties: Walking stick; lunch box; bucket; small box (releasing white "smoke" when opened).

Setting: Scene 1, on the shore, near a little town in Japan. There is a boat center, and a hut, at right. Scene 2, at sea. There is a sky backdrop, and if desired, cardboard waves, which may be moved about to give the effect of a rough ocean. Scenes 3 and 4: The palace of the Dragon King. There is a beautiful throne center stage, and walls are covered with gem-like stones and coral. A thin scrim with net seaweed sewn on it may be draped across the stage to give the effect of being under water. Scene 5, the same as Scene 1, except that hut looks old, with torn screens and the roof falling in.

Lighting: No special effects.

Sound: Gong; howling of wind; Japanese music, as indicated in text.

TOADS AND DIAMONDS

A dramatization from Perrault's tales

Characters

WIDOW, *a bad-tempered woman*
FANNY, *her ill-bred daughter*
GRACE, *her sweet, good daughter*
OLD WOMAN
PRINCESS
PRINCE
KITTY, *non-speaking part*

SCENE 1

SETTING: *Exterior of a small French cottage, with opening for door.*
AT RISE: GRACE *is playing with* KITTY.

GRACE: Here, kitty! (*To herself*) I've been up since four o'clock this morning, and I've finished with my housework. I don't think Mother and my sister, Fanny, are up yet, so I have time to play a little. Here, kitty! (KITTY *meows, and* GRACE *laughs.*) You are such a cute little kitten!
WIDOW (*Appearing at door of cottage*): Grace! What are you doing? My breakfast isn't made yet. (FANNY *comes out of the house.*)
FANNY (*Sarcastically*): Dear sister! Come here at once and comb my hair. (WIDOW *enters.*) Mother, why does she play with that foolish cat? She should get rid of it, and

spend more time caring for the house. (FANNY *re-enters house*.)

GRACE: But, Mother, I've been up since four and I've scrubbed the floors, washed the windows, and hung out the wash.

WIDOW: There is still the baking to do, and polishing and dusting.

FANNY (*Coming out of house, carrying empty water jar*): Look, Mother. The water jar is empty. How can I wash my face without any water?

WIDOW: Grace! Go immediately to the well and get some water. And come right back.

GRACE: But, Mother, it is a good hour's walk to the well in the woods.

WIDOW: You'll just have to hurry, then. We don't have all day.

GRACE: Yes, Mother. I'll be back as soon as I can. (*She takes jar and exits*.)

FANNY: Such a stupid girl! I don't know why we put up with her.

WIDOW (*Slyly*): Perhaps we won't have to much longer, Fanny. She will get her just deserts. (*Curtain*)

*   *   *

SCENE 2

SETTING: *The woods. There is a well, center.*

AT RISE: OLD WOMAN *sits by the well.* GRACE *enters, carrying water jar.*

GRACE: Hello, old woman.

OLD WOMAN: I am so thirsty. I have walked all night and cannot take another step.

GRACE: Let me help you. Here, I will get you a drink of cool water. (*She dips her jar into the well.*)
OLD WOMAN: That is so kind of you, my dear.
GRACE: Here you are. Drink. (OLD WOMAN *drinks from jar.*) Now, don't you feel refreshed?
OLD WOMAN: Thank you very much. You are so thoughtful. What is your name?
GRACE: My name is Grace. I live in a town far from here.
OLD WOMAN: Do you come to this well every day?
GRACE: Yes. Neither my sister nor my mother will ever fetch the water.
OLD WOMAN: What do they do?
GRACE: They sleep until noon and then I give them their breakfast. Then they must bathe and dress. Then I serve lunch. Then . . .
OLD WOMAN (*Dismayed*): It seems as if you do all the work.
GRACE: Yes, but I don't mind. I have nothing else to do.
OLD WOMAN: You speak such sweet words, child. When you go home, you will be rewarded. With every word you speak, either a flower or a jewel shall come out of your mouth.
GRACE: Wouldn't that be amazing. Thank you for your kind thoughts. (OLD WOMAN *disappears.*) Oh! She's gone. What could have happened to her? Oh, well, I must hurry home now, or Mother will be very upset with me. (*She exits with jar. Curtain*)

*   *   *

SCENE 3

SETTING: *Same as Scene 1.*
AT RISE: WIDOW *and* FANNY *come out of cottage.*

WIDOW (*Calling*): Grace! Grace! Now, where can that lazy girl be?

FANNY: She knows that I can't wash my face without clean, pure water. All we have is rain water, and you know what that does to my beautiful face.

WIDOW (*Looking carefully at* FANNY): Hmmm. Yes — you should use fresh water. You are right. Too much rain water is spoiling your beauty.

FANNY: What are you saying? Do you mean to tell me that my skin is not perfect?

WIDOW: No, of course not. You are as beautiful as I am. (GRACE *rushes in, with jar.*)

FANNY: Here's Grace now.

WIDOW: Where have you been, you lazy thing? It's been more than an hour since you went for the water.

FANNY (*Taking jar; angrily*): Half the water is gone. What am I going to use to wash my face?

GRACE: I'm sorry. I hurried as fast as I could, but I'm afraid that when I climbed over the rocks, a little of the water spilled out. (*As she speaks, diamonds, pearls and flowers come out of her mouth.*)

FANNY (*Amazed*): Mother! Look! Diamonds, pearls and flowers are coming out of Grace's mouth!

WIDOW: Goodness! How is this happening? It is magic, a spell. She must be a witch.

GRACE: I am not a witch, Mother. (*More diamonds, pearls and flowers come out.*)

FANNY: I cannot believe it! What's happening?

GRACE: I met an old woman by the well, and gave her a drink of water. (*More diamonds, etc., come out.*)

WIDOW: Was that all that happened?

GRACE: That was all. (*More diamonds come out.*)

WIDOW: Hmmm, I see. Well, tomorrow Fanny shall go to get the water from the well.

FANNY (*Surprised*): Mother! I never go to the well.

WIDOW: Fanny, dear. Don't you want to speak in such beautiful tones?

FANNY (*Suddenly realizing*): Oh . . . I understand. Of course. Tomorrow I shall go for the water. (*Chuckles*)

WIDOW: Now, girls, go inside. Grace, prepare our dinner, and talk as much as you want. As much as you want. (*They all go into house. Curtain*)

* * *

SCENE 4

SETTING: *Same as Scene 2.*

AT RISE: FANNY *enters, carrying water jar.*

FANNY: Oh . . . my poor, poor feet. I can't go another step. Here is the well, but where is the old woman? Not here. (*Angrily*) I walked all this way only to find no one! When I return home, I'll make my sister answer to me for this! (PRINCESS *appears.*)

PRINCESS: Good day, my good woman.

FANNY (*Testily*): Who are you, and what do you want? Did you see an old woman here about?

PRINCESS: I'm afraid I didn't. I was wondering if you could give me a sip of water from your water jar.

FANNY (*Insolently*): Get your own water jar. I don't have time to serve you. You don't see me asking for help. You probably have servants galore that wait on you hand and foot. I only have my stupid sister, Grace, to wait on me. But she is never fast enough. And she always pulls my hair when she combs it.

PRINCESS: You are not very helpful, I must say — and rather rude.

FANNY: I'll say what I wish to say. I'm here to get a present from an old woman.

PRINCESS: Oh, I see. You are waiting for a present. Then hear what I have to say. I am that old woman you are seeking. (PRINCESS *turns into* OLD WOMAN.)

OLD WOMAN: And this is the gift I will give you: With every word you speak, a snake or a toad shall come out of your mouth.

FANNY: No! You can't do this to me! (*Toad comes out of* FANNY'*s mouth.*)

OLD WOMAN: Now, go home and show your mother your gift. (FANNY *runs off, leaving jar behind.* OLD WOMAN *disappears. Curtain*)

*   *   *

SCENE 5

SETTING: *Same as Scene 1.*
AT RISE: FANNY *enters.*

FANNY: Hmmmmmmm. Hmmmm.

WIDOW (*Running out of cottage*): Fanny! Is that you? Where is your water jar?

FANNY: Hmmm. Hmmm.

WIDOW: Did you find the old woman?

FANNY:Hmmm. Hmmm.

WIDOW: Speak up, Fanny! Did you get the gift from the old woman? Do you speak with diamonds, pearls and flowers?

GRACE (*Coming out*): Poor Fanny. Look at her feet, Mother. They are bruised. (*Diamonds and flowers come out.*)

FANNY (*Pointing at* GRACE): It is all her fault, Mother. (*Toads and snakes come out of* FANNY's *mouth.*) Grace made this happen to me. (*Toads and snakes come out.*)

WIDOW (*Screaming*): Oh, Fanny! What happened to you? Look! Toads and snakes are coming out of your mouth!

FANNY: Oh, Mother! (*More toads and snakes come out.*)

WIDOW: Grace! This is all your fault, you nasty girl. Leave at once. Go away and never return. (*She comforts* FANNY.) My poor, poor little girl.

GRACE: But I didn't do anything wrong! (*Diamonds and flowers come out.*)

WIDOW: Go!

GRACE: Goodbye, then . . . Mother . . . dear . . . (*Diamonds, pearls and flowers come out as* GRACE *exits. Curtain*)

*   *   *

SCENE 6

SETTING: *Same as Scene 2.*
AT RISE: GRACE *enters.*

GRACE (*Crying*): Oh, dear. What shall I do? I have no home now. This well is the only other place I know. What shall I do? (*As she cries, diamonds and flowers come out.*)

PRINCE (*Entering; to audience*): Who is this? What a beautiful young woman. And look at all those beautiful gems and flowers about her. She must be enchanted. (*To* GRACE) Who are you, my dear?

GRACE: I am but a poor country girl, sent away from home, and I'm all alone. (*Diamonds and flowers come out.*)

PRINCE: Well, you may be a country girl and alone, but you certainly aren't poor.

GRACE: What do you mean? (*Diamonds and flowers come out.*)

PRINCE: Why, your gift of speaking diamonds, pearls and flowers makes you rich.

GRACE (*Surprised*): Do you mean these things are valuable?

PRINCE: You truly have a dowry worthy of a princess. Your beauty and humble qualities are more valuable than any jewel or flower to me. Won't you marry me and help rule the kingdom? We will live happily ever after in my castle. (*A castle on a hill, glittering in the sun, is revealed at back.*)

GRACE (*Overcome*): Your Highness! I would like that very much. (*A stream of diamonds, pearls, and flowers come out of* GRACE's *mouth as they exit. Curtain*)

THE END

Toads and Diamonds

Production Notes

Number of Puppets: 7 hand or rod puppets, or marionettes. Note: When Princess "changes" back into Old Woman, Princess puppet can simply be replaced with Old Woman puppet at the appropriate time, or a marionette with a different head at each end can be flipped over.

Playing Time: 20 minutes.

Costumes: French country clothes of the 18th century. Consult costume books or fairytale books for suggestions. To create the "magic" effects — diamonds, pearls and flowers coming out of Grace's mouth, toads and snakes out of Fanny's — sparkling "gems" and toad and snake cut-outs can be strung on cord and threaded into the hollow heads of the two puppets. Pull the cords out of the puppets' mouths at the right time.

Properties: An empty water jar.

Setting: Scenes 1, 3 and 5: Backdrop showing house, a half-timbered cottage with a straw roof. There is an opening for the door. Many flowers grow around the cottage. Scenes 2, 4, and 6: The forest, with a well at center. Leave this scene in place during the show and lower house backdrop over it, as indicated. At end of play, backdrop showing castle on a hill can be lowered.

Lighting: No special effects.

Sound: Cry of cat, as indicated.

UNCLE REMUS TALES

Adapted from the stories of Joel Chandler Harris

Characters

UNCLE REMUS
JOHNNY, *a little boy*
GINNY, *a little girl*
BRER RABBIT
BRER FOX
BRER BEAR
BRER TERRAPIN, *a turtle*

SCENE 1

BEFORE RISE: UNCLE REMUS *enters in front of curtain, smoking his pipe. He begins to cross the stage, as* JOHNNY *and* GINNY *enter.*

JOHNNY: Look, Ginny! There's Uncle Remus.
GINNY: I wonder if he would tell us one of his wonderful stories.
JOHNNY: He's a good friend of mine. I'll ask him. (*Calls*) Uncle Remus!
REMUS (*Stopping; turning*): Hello there, Johnny! And there is your friend, Ginny. It's good to see you children.
JOHNNY: Uncle Remus, would you tell us one of your stories?
GINNY: You tell such good ones.

REMUS (*Laughing*): It's just about that time of day when a story would be right. Come sit down and I'll think up a good one. (JOHNNY *and* GINNY *sit next to* REMUS, *stage right.*) Now, let's see! Have you heard the one about Brer Fox and his goobers? Those are peanuts to you.

JOHNNY: No, you haven't told us that one, Uncle Remus.

REMUS: Then, get ready. Here it comes. There was one season when Brer Fox took a notion to plant a goober patch.

*   *   *

SETTING: *Goober patch. There is a patch of peanut plants surrounded by a fence. A tree with rope attached to it is at one side.*

AT RISE: *Curtain opens.* BRER FOX *enters.* REMUS, GINNY, *and* JOHNNY *remain onstage, watching.*

BRER FOX (*Singing or chanting*):
> Time to plant the goobers—
> It's this season's chore.
> Rows and rows of peanuts—
> Time for nuts galore.
> Put them in the ground, so
> They'll grow more and more.
> Sow the tasty peanuts—
> Plant them nice and thick.
> Wait a couple weeks, then
> They'll be right to pick.

Boy, oh, boy. Goobers! When these goobers are ripe, they are going to be mine — all mine. And I'm making sure nobody else is going to get them. I've put up a fence, and that'll keep out thieves. (*Exits*)

REMUS: But once the goobers came up out of the ground, Brer Rabbit took a few of them. (*Peanut plants "grow" up out of stage.* BRER RABBIT *enters with bag and pretends to pick them.*)

BRER RABBIT: Yum, yum. Goobers! (*He runs off.*)

REMUS: Boy, is Brer Fox going to be mad! Let's see what happens next, children. (REMUS, JOHNNY, *and* GINNY *exit.*)

BRER FOX (*Entering and singing*):
        Time to pick the goobers—
        Time to take them home.
        Store them up for winter,
        When I cannot roam.

Now to pick those peanuts. (*Walks to peanut patch, as peanut plants "disappear" under stage*) Hey, somebody else has picked them first! (*Growls*) Gr-r-r! That makes me mad. I'll bet Brer Rabbit took my goobers. Now, where did he break in? (*Looks around*) Aha! There's a hole in that fence. (*Angrily*) I'll set a trap and catch him. (*Going to tree*) I'll bend down this tree and tie this rope to one end. (*He pulls tree over, using rope.*) Then I'll make a loop at the other end and tie it to the hole in the fence. (*Rope is attached to fence.*) I'll catch that old rabbit. Just wait and see! (*Laughs*) This is the end of Brer Rabbit. I'll have him caught in no time. (*Exits, laughing*)

BRER RABBIT (*Looking out from side of stage*): Guess it's all right for me to come out now. Brer Fox isn't here. (*He enters, carrying bag.*) Look here. More goobers! Yum, yum. I'll climb through this hole in the fence. (*Gets caught in rope, and is pulled up into tree*) Oh, no! Brer Fox has caught me in one of his silly old traps. (*Struggling*) Ugh! I can't budge. I'm caught tight. Oh, oh! I hear someone coming. (BEAR *enters and* RABBIT *calls to him.*) Hi there, Brer Bear!

BRER BEAR: Who's that? (*Looks up at tree*) Why, it's Brer Rabbit! What are you doing up there?

BRER RABBIT (*Innocently*): Who, me? Oh, I'm working on a job.

BRER BEAR: What sort of work can you do up there?

BRER RABBIT: Scarecrow sort of work. I'm keeping the crows out of Brer Fox's goober patch. Brer Fox is paying me a lot of money for this work.

BRER BEAR: How much is he paying you?

BRER RABBIT: A gold piece a minute! Did you ever earn a gold piece a minute, Brer Bear?

BRER BEAR: No, Brer Rabbit. I never have.

BRER RABBIT (*Slyly*): Wouldn't you like to make a gold piece a minute?

BRER BEAR: No, thank you, Brer Rabbit. I don't know anything about scarecrow work.

BRER RABBIT: It's easy to do, Brer Bear. There's nothing to it! And, all the time you're up in this tree, the gold pieces just pile up. Big, round gold pieces. Wouldn't you like to earn some?

BRER BEAR: No, no! I couldn't take away your job. Those gold pieces should go to you.

BRER RABBIT: But I have so many, Brer Bear. My chimney is just stuffed up with them. Is your chimney stuffed up with gold pieces, Brer Bear?

BRER BEAR: Oh, no! It isn't stuffed at all.

BRER RABBIT (*Cajoling*): Wouldn't you like to buy yourself something sweet? You can buy all the sweets you want with this gold.

BRER BEAR: I love sweets. I wish I had some right now.

BRER RABBIT: Well, then, you have to get some gold pieces — quick. I'll have to let you take over this scarecrow job now — this very minute.

BRER BEAR: That's mighty nice of you, Brer Rabbit. You

are right. I should get some gold pieces — quick. (*He goes to tree and takes down* RABBIT.) I can hardly wait to get up in that tree to take your place.

BRER RABBIT: Here, let me help you. Just bend down this tree. (*They bend tree, and* BEAR *gets on it.*) Now, put your feet in the rope, and let go of the tree. (*The tree straightens, and* BEAR *is pulled up with it.*) There! Are you comfortable? (RABBIT *sits on fence.*)

BRER BEAR: Why, yes, Brer Rabbit. (FOX *enters with stick.*)

BRER RABBIT: Howdy, Brer Fox. Looks as if Brer Bear's been stealing your goobers. I see you have him caught in your trap.

BRER FOX: Brer Bear! Why, that pesky good-for-nothing, I'm going to give him the worst licking of his life. (*He hits* BEAR *with a stick.*) Take that, you lazy bear.

BRER BEAR (*Crying out*): Ouch! Ouch! Wait, Brer Fox. Wait! You forgot the gold pieces! Ouch! Ouch! (RABBIT *gathers peanuts and puts them into his bag, then exits.*)

BRER FOX (*Continuing to hit* BEAR): Thief! Goober stealer! Take that. And that!

BRER BEAR: Ouch! Please stop.

REMUS (*Entering and closing curtains*): Poor Brer Bear took a beating from Brer Fox, and Brer Rabbit got away with more of Brer Fox's goobers. (*Laughs*) He sure is one smart rabbit. But Brer Fox learned who really stole his goobers, and then he was determined to catch Brer Rabbit. (REMUS *remains onstage.*)

*   *   *

SCENE 2

BEFORE RISE: JOHNNY *and* GINNY *enter.*

JOHNNY: That was a good story, Uncle Remus.

GINNY: Can you tell us another one? There's still some time.

REMUS: Well, the sun hasn't quite set yet, so let me see. Hm-m-m. Here's a story you'll like. It's called, ''The Moon in the Mill Pond.'' One night Brer Rabbit and Brer Terrapin were over by the mill pond. They were singing about old times, sitting by the warm campfire. (*They exit. Curtain opens.*)

*   *   *

SETTING: *A mill in the distance by a pond, and a bright, full moon above, reflecting in pond. A campfire is at center.*

AT RISE: BRER RABBIT *and* BRER TERRAPIN *sit around the fire.* TERRAPIN *is playing his banjo. Sound of banjo music is heard from offstage. They may sing an appropriate folksong.*

BRER RABBIT: It's good to sit under the moon with nothing to worry about.

BRER TERRAPIN: How about your enemies, Brer Fox and Brer Bear? Aren't you worried about them?

BRER RABBIT: Yes, but they're probably sound asleep by this time. (*A tapping sound is heard from offstage.*)

BRER TERRAPIN (*Suddenly*): What's that? I heard something.

BRER RABBIT (*Not worried*): It's just a frog jumping in the mill pond. (FOX *and* BEAR *enter, unnoticed, and sneak across the stage behind them.*) We have nothing to fear.

BEAR TERRAPIN (*Seeing them and pointing*): There they are! (*Excited*) It's Brer Fox and Brer Bear! Sure as you live, they're planning to nab and roast us for dinner — right here by our campfire.

BRER RABBIT: Sh-h-h. Don't get riled up. I have an idea. (*Loudly*) This fire has to be just hot enough, but not too hot — because we have a real feast to cook tonight. (FOX and BEAR *come to front near* RABBIT *and* TERRAPIN. RABBIT *pretends to be surprised.*) Bless my soul, if it isn't Brer Fox and Brer Bear! We're surely glad to see you. Why, just this very minute Brer Terrapin and I were wondering how we were going to eat our big dinner all alone. Would you like to eat with us?

BRER FOX (*Looking around; suspiciously*): I don't see any big dinner.

BRER RABBIT: Of course, you don't see the dinner now — but you wait.

BRER BEAR: Where are you getting this big dinner?

BRER RABBIT (*Pointing to mill pond*): Right down at the mill pond. Sh-h-h! It's waiting there, this very minute. The finest mess of fish in all the world.

BRER BEAR: What kind of fish?

BRER RABBIT: The juiciest, most delicious fish you ever ate.

BRER FOX: Hm-m-m! How are you going to catch the fish? I don't see any fishing line and I don't see any fishing pole.

BRER RABBIT (*Bragging*): Why, catching them is easy. These fish aren't ordinary fish. On a night like this, when the moon's up there in the sky, these fish come right to the top of the water, and they dance. Sometimes you can even hear them — ''Hippity, flippity; hippity, flippity.'' All you have to do is reach down with your paw, and scoop them up. Come on, everybody. It's getting late and I'm getting hungry. Let's go get the fish now. (RABBIT *and* TERRAPIN *go to one side of the stage.*)

BRER FOX (*Whispering to* BEAR): We might as well get our

share of these fish, too. We can roast up Brer Rabbit and Brer Terrapin later for dessert. (*They laugh.*)

BRER BEAR: Good idea!

BRER TERRAPIN (*To* **RABBIT**): Brer Rabbit, what are we going to do? You know there are no fish in the mill pond. Brer Fox and Brer Bear are going to eat us instead.

BRER RABBIT: Don't worry, Brer Terrapin. I can handle this. Look at the moon. Do you see its reflection in the water? The moon is shining down from the sky, but it looks as if it is lying at the bottom of the pond. That gives me an idea. (**FOX** *and* **BEAR** *come up to them.*)

BRER FOX: Well, Brer Rabbit. Where are the fish?

BRER RABBIT (*Pretending to be upset*): Brer Fox, Brer Bear — look what happened! (*He points at the pond.*)

BRER BEAR: What in the world is the matter, Brer Rabbit? Why are you staring down into the pond? (*They all look into the pond.*)

BRER RABBIT: Bad . . . . Mighty bad. The moon has dropped down into the pond and scared all the dancing fishes away. Look way, way down, and you'll see the moon there for yourselves.

BRER BEAR (*Looking down*): Sure enough. There lies the moon, swinging and swaying at the very bottom of the pond. This surely is bad luck. (*He growls.*)

BRER FOX: It sure is. (*Grumbles*) Gr-r-r!

BRER RABBIT: Unless we get that moon out of this pond, we aren't going to have any fish for our dinner tonight.

BRER FOX: How are we going to do that?

BRER RABBIT: How? Well, I expect the best way to catch the moon is to use a fishing net. I'll go get one. (*He exits.*)

BRER TERRAPIN: There are more strange doings around

this mill pond than most folks know. But I know, and the lizards know, and the bullfrogs know. Yes, we all know about that pot of gold.

BRER FOX *and* **BRER BEAR** (*Excited; shouting*): What pot of gold?

BRER TERRAPIN: There's a pot of gold at the bottom of the pond — it's right under the moon. Sh-h-h! Here comes Brer Rabbit. Don't say a word to him about this.

BRER RABBIT (*Returning, with a net*): Here's the net. Now to catch the moon. I'll just jump into the pond.

BRER FOX: Wait, Brer Rabbit! Let Brer Bear and me trap the moon for you.

BRER BEAR: Yes, we want to do it. Get out of our way! (*They grab the net from* **RABBIT**, *push him aside, and "jump" into the water. A splash is heard from offstage.*) Br-r-r! That's cold.

BRER FOX: Br-r-r! It sure is.

BRER RABBIT (*Shouting*): Spread out the net, and drag it back and forth through the water.

BRER FOX: Are we out far enough?

BRER RABBIT: Keep going out. And remember to drag the net back and forth across the pond.

BRER BEAR: But we're not catching anything. Where's the moon? Where's the gold?

BRER FOX (*To* **BEAR**): Sh-h-h! Don't mention the gold.

BRER RABBIT: You haven't gone out far enough. Go out still farther.

BRER FOX: Out here, Brer Rabbit? Right here? (**FOX** *and* **BEAR** *suddenly "disappear" beneath the stage.*) Oh, no! The water's deep here. Help! Help!

BRER BEAR (*Yelling*): We're out too far. Help us! (**BEAR** *and* **FOX** *make gulping and bubbling noises.*)

BRER FOX: We're getting tangled in the net. Help! Help!

Brer Rabbit (*Slyly*): You mean you haven't caught the moon yet?

Brer Terrapin: And you haven't found the gold? Well, keep trying. (**Rabbit** *and* **Terrapin** *laugh and run off.* **Remus** *enters and closes curtain.*)

Remus: Brer Rabbit and Brer Terrapin are safe again from Brer Bear and Brer Fox, I guess. (**Ginny** *and* **Johnny** *enter.*)

Johnny: Did Brer Fox and Brer Bear ever get out of the pond?

Remus: Oh, yes, they finally swam to shore, but they didn't catch the moon . . . or find the gold, either. (*He laughs, then looks up.*) Well, the sun has set — your folks will be looking for you.

Ginny *and* **Johnny** (*Together*): Goodbye, Uncle Remus. (*They exit.*)

Remus: Goodbye. (*To audience*) And goodbye to you, everybody. Come visit Uncle Remus again, you hear. (*He laughs and exits.*)

THE END

Uncle Remus Tales

PRODUCTION NOTES

Number of Puppets: 7 hand or rod puppets, or marionettes.

Playing Time: 20 minutes.

Costumes: Animals may wear trousers and shirts and even funny hats. Use your imagination. Uncle Remus is black and should have gray hair. He can wear overalls, a shirt, and an old hat. The children are in play clothes.

Properties: Pipe; stick; bag; fishing net; banjo.

Setting: Scene 1: Goober patch, surrounded by a fence. Tree with rope attached to it is at one side. Scene 2: A pond, with a bright, full moon above. A mill is in the distance, and a campfire is at center. Painted sets can be used for both scenes, and goober plants can be section of scenery that rises from floor.

Lighting: Blue light should shine on the mill pond, to suggest night.

Sound: Tapping; splash; old-time banjo music or folk music, as indicated in text.

MANORA, THE BIRD PRINCESS

A tale of ancient Siam

Characters

PRINCE RAMA
KING NAGA, *a snake*
MANORA, *the bird princess*
ROCHANA, *her sister*
MAKULA, *her other sister*
KING RUANG, *Rama's father*
PRIME MINISTER
FISH
BIRD
BIRD KING, *Manora's father*
NARRATOR

SCENE 1

SETTING: *A forest near the shore of a lake.*
AT RISE: *The snake,* KING NAGA, *is twisted around a tree.*

NARRATOR: Long ago, in a golden city at the top of the Phanom Dong Raek Mountains in Thailand, there lived a king of the bird people and his three beautiful daughters. Every full moon the three princesses would fly to a lake deep in the forest where they would swim in the refreshing waters until dawn. One evening as they were bathing in the lake . . .
PRINCE RAMA (*Entering and peering offstage*): What is this I see before me? Are my eyes deceiving me? Three lovely

109

bird creatures swimming in the lake. Where did they come from? Who could they be?

KING NAGA: Hs-s-t! Help me, young prince, and I will tell you what you wish to know.

PRINCE RAMA (*Turning*): Why, who are you? How can I help you?

KING NAGA: I am Naga, the serpent king of the forest. I have wound myself into a knot around this tree and cannot untie myself.

PRINCE RAMA: Here — let me help you. (*He releases* KING NAGA.) There!

KING NAGA: Thank you, Prince Rama. The animals of the forest say you are kind, and I can see that it is true. I would like to help you, to show my gratitude.

PRINCE RAMA: Then, please tell me about those beautiful birds that I see near the lake.

KING NAGA: They are princesses — daughters of the Bird King.

PRINCE RAMA: And that one closest to the shore. She is so beautiful! What is her name?

KING NAGA: I believe that is Manora, but I am not certain, for all three princesses look very much alike.

PRINCE RAMA: Ah, but that one especially intrigues me. Would she speak to me, do you think?

KING NAGA: No — the bird people do not trust human beings.

PRINCE RAMA: Perhaps she might listen to me, if I could catch her.

KING NAGA: Hm-m-m. Perhaps. Here, take this magic wand. (*Wand appears.*) Whoever is touched by the wand will become your prisoner for as long as you wish.

PRINCE RAMA (*Taking wand*): Oh, thank you, King Naga! And how may I repay you for your generosity?

KING NAGA: You already have, my dear prince. You already have. (*Hisses*) Ss-s-s! Good day. I must be on my way now.

PRINCE RAMA: Goodbye, King Naga, and thank you. (KING NAGA *exits.*)

MANORA (*From offstage*): Sisters! Makula! Rochana! I am going to rest for a while over there. We should leave for home soon. It is almost dawn.

PRINCE RAMA (*To himself*): What luck! I see Manora coming this way. I shall hide from her. (*He exits.*)

MANORA (*Entering*): How cool it is here in the forest! This looks like a peaceful spot to rest.

PRINCE RAMA (*Jumping onstage and touching her with wand*): Ahhhh—now I have you!

MANORA (*In alarm*): Oh, who are you? What have you done? I cannot move!

PRINCE RAMA: I am Prince Rama, and I have made you my prisoner because I wish to talk with you. I think that I have fallen in love with you, beautiful princess.

MANORA: But I do not know you, and I fear all human beings.

PRINCE RAMA: Do not be afraid of me, Manora. I will not harm you.

MANORA: You do seem kind.

PRINCE RAMA: Will you come to live in a small cottage near my palace? You have only to stay there for one year — if at the end of that time you have not grown to love me, you may return home.

MANORA: All right, Prince Rama. I will go with you. (*Two other bird princesses,* ROCHANA *and* MAKULA, *enter, "flying."*)

ROCHANA: Sister, are you all right? Who is this man?

MANORA: This is Prince Rama, Rochana.

MAKULA: Has he harmed you?

MANORA: No, no, Makula! He means no harm. It is almost dawn, and Father will be worried. You must return home and tell him that I will be gone for a year.

ROCHANA (*Surprised*): What do you mean, sister?

MAKULA: Are you ever coming home again?

MANORA: Yes, I shall return — either alone, or with a husband.

MAKULA: How romantic! (*She giggles.*)

MANORA: Hush, silly one. Now, be off!

ROCHANA: Goodbye, Manora.

MAKULA: And be careful! Remember — he is a human. (MAKULA *and* ROCHANA *laugh as they* "*fly*" *off. Curtain.*)

*　　*　　*

SCENE 2

TIME: *Almost a year later.*

SETTING: *Prince Rama's palace garden. Beautiful flowering bushes are at either side.*

AT RISE: MANORA *is onstage.* PRINCE RAMA *enters.*

PRINCE RAMA: Ah, Manora! There you are. I was hoping I would find you here. I'm afraid I have some bad news.

MANORA: What is it, Prince?

PRINCE RAMA: An army from Burma is attacking the borders of my kingdom. I must leave immediately to protect my land.

MANORA: How sad, my prince! I shall miss you.

PRINCE RAMA: You will? How sweet those words sound to me! Remember, your year is almost over. When I return from the war, I shall expect an answer from you concerning our marriage.

MANORA: I shall be ready to give you my answer then, my prince.

PRINCE RAMA: Farewell, sweet Manora. (*Calling*) Prime Minister, prepare my horse — I must leave at once!

PRIME MINISTER (*Entering*): Yes, Your Highness. Right away, Your Highness! (*He exits.*)

MANORA: Please return safely.

PRINCE RAMA: Fear not. (*Pantomimes handing ring to* MANORA) Here — take my ring and wear it to bring me luck.

MANORA: I shall wear it forever.

PRIME MINISTER (*Entering with prop horse*): Your horse is ready, Your Highness.

PRINCE RAMA (*Mounting horse*): Remember, Manora, I shall expect your answer when I return. Goodbye! (*He gallops off.*)

MANORA: Goodbye! Oh, how happy he will be when I give him my answer.

PRIME MINISTER: What answer is that, Princess Manora?

MANORA: Why, that I shall accept his proposal of marriage — and will gladly become his wife.

PRIME MINISTER: Oh—ah—yes, of course.

MANORA: I have learned to love him for his brave and gentle ways.

PRIME MINISTER: Hm-m-m. (*Pointing to bush*) Do you see that beautiful flower over there? It would look lovely in your hair. Why don't you pick it?

MANORA (*Going to bush*): Oh, my! It really is beautiful, isn't it? But, do you think I should pick it? The King is very proud of these gardens.

PRIME MINISTER: Nonsense, my dear. Pick it, pick it! The King won't mind.

MANORA: All right, if you say so. It is beautiful. (*Picks the flower*) There.

PRIME MINISTER: Lovely, lovely!

MANORA: I shall wear it in my hair tonight.

PRIME MINISTER: Why don't you put it on now and see how you look in your mirror?

MANORA: What a fine idea! I shall return to my cottage right away, and try it on. (*Exits*)

PRIME MINISTER (*Suddenly evil*): Ha, ha! The little fool! So she thinks *she* is going to marry the Prince, eh? We'll see! She won't if I can help it. It is my daughter who will marry the Prince, not a common little bird princess.

KING RUANG (*Entering*): Ah, Prime Minister, admiring my beautiful garden, are you?

PRIME MINISTER: Well — er, no, Your Majesty. I was just noticing that someone has picked a blossom from your hibiscus. See how clumsily they have broken it off!

KING RUANG: Why, look at that. How terrible!

PRIME MINISTER: And it was Your Majesty's own order that anyone who picks these flowers would be locked in the tower and kept there.

KING RUANG: That's right. I said that, didn't I?

PRIME MINISTER: So you did, Your Majesty. So you did!

MANORA (*Entering with the flower in her hair*): You were right. See how lovely the flower looks in my hair!

PRIME MINISTER: Aha! There's the culprit. Look at her! She has your hibiscus in her hair.

MANORA (*Puzzled*): You said that I should wear it.

PRIME MINISTER: Remember your law, Your Majesty.

KING RUANG: Manora! You disobeyed my order. I'm afraid I'll have to have you locked away in the tower.

MANORA: But, I only did what seemed right.

PRIME MINISTER: Enough — enough. I will have her chained and taken away.

KING RUANG: Do you have any last requests, Manora, before we carry out your punishment?

MANORA: Your Majesty! Forgive me if I have done something to offend you. I should like to make amends by dancing for you one last time.

KING RUANG: How sweet of you, Manora. You know how fond I am of your bird dances. This should be a pleasure. (*Music is heard offstage, as* MANORA *begins to dance. Suddenly she "flies" above stage.*)

MANORA: Farewell, King.

PRIME MINISTER: Stop her! Stop her! Come back!

MANORA: I am returning to my father. Tell Prince Rama that I really do love him.

KING RUANG: Farewell, Princess Manora. You have saved me from carrying out a very unpleasant duty. (MANORA *"flies" off. Curtain*)

*　　　*　　　*

SCENE 3

TIME: *Three years later.*

SETTING: *A dark forest. There is a river, with a large rock and mountain near its banks.*

AT RISE: PRINCE RAMA *enters.*

NARRATOR: When Prince Rama returned home successfully from the wars, he discovered that his bird princess had gone. He left the palace at once to search for her.

PRINCE RAMA: For over three years now I have looked for Manora, but have found no sign of her. (*Looks up at mountain*) The top of the mountain is said to be the home of the bird people. Looking there is my last hope, but the rock is too steep to climb. What shall I do? Must I admit defeat? (*Bravely*) No, I shall go on until my last breath. I shall never accept anything less than victory.

KING NAGA (*Appearing*): Ss-s-t! Well said, Prince Rama. It seems that I may be able to help you again.

PRINCE RAMA: Ah, King Naga, my old friend. How good to see you again!

KING NAGA: In order to reach the kingdom of the bird people, you must enter the mountain through a cave, somewhere in this forest. Here. (*Pantomimes giving whistle*) Take this magic whistle. Blow it once, and all the fish of the river will come to your aid. Blow it twice, and all the birds of the forest will help you.

PRINCE RAMA: Thank you, King Naga. I shall always remember your kindness. (KING NAGA *exits.*) Now, to find that cave which leads to the mountaintop. What is this strange-looking rock over here? (*He goes to large rock.*) It looks as if it has been put there to cover something. I wonder if I can move it. (*He pushes rock and it moves, revealing an entrance to a cave.*) Why, I've found the cave! How lucky I am! I shall see if it leads to the top of the mountain, as King Naga said it would. (*He enters cave, and rock closes. Curtain*)

*   *   *

SCENE 4

TIME: *Later that day.*

SETTING: *Inside the palace of the Bird King. A throne is at center.*

AT RISE: BIRD KING *sits on his throne.* MANORA *is nearby.*

BIRD KING: Do not be so sad, Manora. Your prince will find you someday soon, if he loves you as much as he told you he did.

MANORA: I know, Father. But not knowing where he is makes me very unhappy. If only I had some news!

ROCHANA (*"Flying" in*): Father, Father! The guards have captured an intruder and have brought him to the palace.

BIRD KING: So! Let us have a look at this trespasser! Have him sent to me immediately!

ROCHANA: Yes, Father. (*She "flies" off.*)

BIRD KING: Manora, I wish to question this man alone. You had better go.

MANORA: Yes, Father. (*She exits.*)

PRINCE RAMA (*Entering*): Forgive me for this intrusion, Your Majesty, but I seek your daughter, Manora. I have been traveling for years, trying to find her.

BIRD KING: And what is it you wish of my daughter?

PRINCE RAMA: I seek her hand in marriage, Your Majesty. I love her very much.

BIRD KING: But how can I be sure of this? Would you be willing to undergo three tests to prove your love?

PRINCE RAMA: I will do anything, Your Majesty. Anything that would bring Manora and me together again.

BIRD KING: Very well! First, you must find one of my favorite crowns, which I lost while crossing the Chaupaya River. It fell from my head into the muddy waters and sank to the bottom.

PRINCE RAMA: I will bring it to you, Your Majesty. What is the second test?

BIRD KING: You must bring back many feathers of brilliant colors for a marriage cape.

PRINCE RAMA: A marriage cape? Would this be for me?

BIRD KING: Yes. It is required in our kingdom that a bridegroom wear a beautiful, feathered cape, and the groom of a princess must wear one that is ten feet long.

PRINCE RAMA: Ten feet! I will need millions of feathers.

BIRD KING: If you really love my daughter, you will find a way to get them.

PRINCE RAMA: Hm-m-m! What's the third test?

BIRD KING: I will tell you about that after you successfully complete the first two — if you are able to.

PRINCE RAMA: Very well, Your Majesty. I shall leave immediately.

BIRD KING: Farewell, brave Prince. The best of luck to you.

PRINCE RAMA: Thank you, Your Majesty. I fear I may need it. (*He exits. Curtain*)

* * *

SCENE 5

SETTING: *The dark forest and river, as in Scene 3.*

AT RISE: PRINCE RAMA *enters. He looks into the river.*

PRINCE RAMA: Here is the Chaupaya River that the Bird King was talking about, but it is very muddy. How will I ever find his crown?

KING NAGA (*Appearing*): Ss-s-t! Did you forget so soon about the gift I gave you?

PRINCE RAMA: King Naga! It's you. Do you know what I am seeking?

KING NAGA: Yes, my friend, for I have many messengers who keep me well-informed.

PRINCE RAMA: How will I ever find a crown in such a muddy river?

KING NAGA: Perhaps you can't — but there is one who could.

PRINCE RAMA: You mean the fish! Of course! I'll just blow the whistle you gave me, and he'll come. (*He pantomimes blowing, as sound of whistle is heard.* FISH *appears.*)

FISH: Did you summon me, master?

PRINCE RAMA: Yes! I must find the crown of the Bird King. It lies somewhere at the bottom of your river.

FISH: If it is in the river, we will find it. (FISH *exits, then appears at once with crown.*) No sooner said than done, Your Highness. And a fine crown it is, too.

PRINCE RAMA (*Ecstatic*): Thank you, little fish! I must take this to the Bird King immediately.

FISH: Farewell, master. Good luck. (FISH *exits.*)

KING NAGA: Aren't you forgetting about something, my prince?

PRINCE RAMA: Of course! The second test. I must find millions of brilliant feathers for my marriage cape.

KING NAGA: Why don't you —

PRINCE RAMA: You don't have to tell me! I'll use my whistle. (*He pantomimes blowing twice, as sound of whistle is heard.*)

BIRD (*Appearing in "sky" above* PRINCE RAMA'*s head*): Did you call, master?

PRINCE RAMA: Yes, dear friend. I need millions of colorful feathers for my marriage cape. But I fear —

BIRD: Fear not, master, for it is our moulting season, and getting enough feathers for you should be no trouble at all. (*Calling*) Birds of the forest: Shake off your feathers! Fill our master's needs. (*The sound of birds calling is heard from offstage, as many colorful feathers drop onto stage from above.*)

PRINCE RAMA: The birds have done it. Look at all these feathers! (*To* BIRD) Thank all the birds for me.

BIRD: I will, Your Highness. Farewell. (BIRD *"flies" off.*)

PRINCE RAMA: Now, I must return to the palace of the Bird King. Thank you for your help, King Naga. Farewell.

KING NAGA: Farewell, great Prince Rama. (KING NAGA *and* PRINCE RAMA *exit. Curtain*)

*   *   *

SCENE 6

TIME: *A short while later.*
SETTING: *The Bird King's palace, as in Scene 4.*
AT RISE: BIRD KING *sits on throne and* PRINCE RAMA *enters, wearing cape.*

BIRD KING: You have done very, very well, Prince Rama. I have my crown again, and you have feathers for your marriage cape.
PRINCE RAMA: I am ready for the third test, Your Majesty. What am I to do?
BIRD KING: Simply this: As you know, my daughters all look very much alike. I shall have them dance for you, and if you can pick out Manora on the first try, you shall have her for your wife.
PRINCE RAMA: That's a fair and pleasant test. When will it take place?
BIRD KING: We shall have it now. (*He claps his hands. Music is heard from offstage, as* ROCHANA, MAKULA, *and* MANORA *enter and dance before throne.*)
PRINCE RAMA: I have never seen such beautiful dancing!
BIRD KING (*As music stops*): Now, you must choose Manora.
PRINCE RAMA: Very well. (*Goes to* MANORA) This is Manora, Your Majesty.
MANORA (*Happily*): Father, the Prince has done it! He has chosen me on the first try.

BIRD KING: He must truly love you to be able to pick you out so quickly from your sisters. Now I shall leave you to make preparations for the wedding. You both must have a lot to talk about. Come, daughters. (*He exits, followed by* ROCHANA *and* MAKULA.)

MANORA: My Prince! How did you choose me so quickly? My sisters and I look so very much alike.

PRINCE RAMA: Yes, you're right. But only you, my dearest Manora, were wearing the ring I gave you to bring me luck.

MANORA: The ring, of course! It brought us luck, indeed. I shall wear it forever.

PRINCE RAMA: Do you really love me, then?

MANORA: With all my heart, my sweet prince. (*They embrace. Curtain*)

THE END

Manora, the Bird Princess

PRODUCTION NOTES

Number of Puppets: 10 hand or rod puppets or marionettes. Shadow puppets, which are traditionally part of performances in Thailand, may be used in Scene 1 for the bathing princesses if desired.

Playing Time: 25 minutes.

Costumes: Manora and her sisters have wings that come from their lower backs, and upturned tails. All wear pointed headdresses of gold and jewels. King Naga wears a simple version of the crown. All wear tight trousers and short jackets, in brilliant colors and sparkling fabrics. They are either barefoot or wear sandals. Fish and Bird resemble Siamese toys. Prince Rama's "feather" cape, which is put on for the final scene, should be full and colorful, with an indication of feathers.

Properties: Wand; hibiscus blossom; horse (may be a puppet); throne; crown; loose feathers.

Setting: Forest; palace garden; another forest, near a mountain and river; inside the Bird King's palace. The settings should not overpower the costumes of the puppets. They should be stylized, using bright and colorful designs. Model thrones, buildings, etc., on illustrations of Thailand. The rock formation that moves aside is a cutout, hinged or on a sliding track. The river is imaginary.

Lighting: No special effects.

Sound: Whistle; bird calls; Oriental and/or Thai music, as indicated in text.

THE BLUE WILLOW

A legend of ancient China

Characters

CHANG, *a youth*
KONGSHEE, *a maiden*
LI CHA, *Kongshee's father*
WAHLING, *Chang's mother*
MANDARIN
DOG
CAT
TWO BLUEBIRDS
NARRATOR

SCENE 1

SETTING: *Outside Li Cha and Wahling's houses. There is a bridge between the houses.*
AT RISE: *The stage is empty.* CHANG *enters from* WAHLING's *house and stands on bridge.*

NARRATOR: This is the story of "The Blue Willow," the tale of two young people, Chang and Kongshee, who were in love. Each evening when the sun set they would meet on the Blue Willow Bridge.
CHANG (*Calling*): Kongshee! Kongshee! Where are you? Come out!
KONGSHEE (*Entering from* LI CHA's *house*): Ah, dear Chang! (*Goes to bridge*)

CHANG: Dear Kongshee!

KONGSHEE: We should not meet here anymore. (*Sadly*) Father wants me to marry another.

CHANG: Never! I shall never allow that to happen. We will run away first.

KONGSHEE: That would disgrace my father and he would lose face.

CHANG: He must allow us to marry. We will find a way to convince him.

LI CHA (*From offstage*): Kongshee! Kongshee!

KONGSHEE: There is Father now. I must go. He will be angry if he sees us here.

CHANG: All right. But do not worry. We will find a way. (KONGSHEE *runs into her house.* CHANG *waves and exits.* DOG *enters and sniffs here and there, then exits.* CAT *enters and slinks around.* DOG *re-enters and barks at* CAT. CAT *growls at* DOG, *and they begin to fight, making a lot of noise.* LI CHA *and* WAHLING *enter from their houses and pull the animals apart.*)

WAHLING (*To* CAT): My poor little cat!

LI CHA (*Angrily*): Why don't you keep your cat inside, Wahling?

WAHLING: Why must your dog always chase my cat? You should have him locked up.

LI CHA (*Angrily*): You should have your son locked up for bothering my daughter!

WAHLING (*Hotly*): Keep your daughter at home!

LI CHA: Perhaps we should take down the Blue Willow Bridge.

WAHLING: Perhaps we should, you windbag!

LI CHA: You busy-body! (*They exit into their respective houses. Curtain*)

*   *   *

SCENE 2

SETTING: *Interior of Li Cha's house.*
AT RISE: DOG *enters and sniffs here and there.* KONGSHEE *enters.*

KONGSHEE: Oh, pity me, little dog. Father doesn't want me to see Chang anymore. (*She weeps.* DOG *tries to comfort her.*)
LI CHA (*Entering*): Kongshee. Why do you sit there and cry? I have good news for you. The rich mandarin from the city has come to see you. Here he is now.
MANDARIN (*Entering*): At last! It is good to meet you, Kongshee. I have been eager to see you. (DOG *growls. He bites* MANDARIN's *leg and holds onto it.* MANDARIN *jumps wildly about, pantomiming pain, as* KONGSHEE *and* LI CHA *try to pull* DOG *away.*)
LI CHA: Kongshee, catch your dog—quickly!
KONGSHEE: Yes, Father. (*Calling* DOG) Here, fellow. Come to me. (DOG *goes to* KONGSHEE.)
MANDARIN (*Grimly*): What a nice little dog you have, Kongshee.
LI CHA: Daughter, take your dog away. I wish to talk to our guest.
KONGSHEE: Yes, Father. (*To* DOG) Come along. (*She picks up* DOG *and, as they exit,* DOG *growls.* MANDARIN *steps aside quickly.*)
LI CHA: So you wish to marry my daughter.
MANDARIN: Yes. I am wealthy and handsome, and I think Kongshee would suit me.
LI CHA: I agree. I agree. And I'm sure she would make you an obedient wife as well.
MANDARIN: It is all arranged, then?

LI CHA: Yes, of course. I will call her at once and tell her the good news. (*Calls*) Kongshee! Come here!

KONGSHEE (*Entering*): Yes, Father?

LI CHA: I have good news for you. It has been arranged that you will marry our friend the mandarin. All we must do is set the date.

KONGSHEE (*Startled*): No, Father! How can you expect me to marry one I do not love?

LI CHA (*Surprised*): What is that you say?

MANDARIN (*Offended*): The impudent little wretch!

KONGSHEE: I am in love with Chang, the youth who lives on the other side of the Blue Willow Bridge. We have vowed to be true to each other.

LI CHA (*In disbelief*): What is that you say?

MANDARIN: He is only a common youth. I have never heard of such a thing.

LI CHA: Kongshee! I am disgraced!

KONGSHEE: If you separate us, Chang and I will jump from the Blue Willow Bridge and return as bluebirds to haunt you both, just as the legend says.

LI CHA: Kongshee! You go to your room. (*She exits.*)

MANDARIN: My! She has a strong will. She speaks her mind.

LI CHA: Don't listen to her. She will do as I say. Come — we will make the arrangements for the wedding. (DOG *re-enters and chases* MANDARIN *offstage. Curtain*)

*   *   *

SCENE 3

TIME: *Evening.*

SETTING: *Same as Scene 1.*

AT RISE: *Stage is empty.* KONGSHEE *enters.*

KONGSHEE (*Calling*): Chang!

CHANG (*Entering*): Kongshee!

KONGSHEE: Shh! Be quiet! We must make our plans.

CHANG: Plans? Plans for what?

KONGSHEE: Father wants to marry me to a rich mandarin.

CHANG: Never! We will run away.

KONGSHEE: I have a better idea. I have made two artificial bluebirds.

CHANG: But, why?

KONGSHEE: I told Father that we would jump off the bridge and drown if he separated us, and then return as bluebirds to haunt him, just as the legend goes.

CHANG: We will pretend to jump and they will think we are gone!

KONGSHEE: Yes. We will hide and fly the bluebird puppets over their heads.

CHANG: They will feel sorry for us and forgive us.

KONGSHEE: And wish they hadn't tried to separate us.

CHANG: Let's do it now. Come. We'll go under the bridge. This way. (*He leads* KONGSHEE *to bridge and they hide under it.*)

KONGSHEE (*Giving a loud cry*): Ooooohhhh!

LI CHA (*Entering*): What was that?

WAHLING (*Entering from opposite side*): I heard a cry. What could that be?

LI CHA: It sounded like Kongshee.

WAHLING: What could have happened? (TWO BLUEBIRDS *appear and fly about.*)

LI CHA: Oh, no! (*With dread*) Two bluebirds. They must have jumped from the Blue Willow Bridge, just as Kongshee warned.

WAHLING: Alas! My poor son!

LI CHA: Kongshee! Kongshee! Come back to me. Come back!

KONGSHEE (*From her hiding place; in mysterious tones*): You wanted to separate Chang and me — and so we have gone away. (MANDARIN *enters.*)

CHANG (*Also in mysterious tones*): Just as the legend says . . . we have turned into bluebirds.

WAHLING (*Crying*): My poor Chang!

KONGSHEE: We will never return again.

LI CHA: Oh, Kongshee, my daughter! I should have listened to you and let you follow your heart. If you ever return I would let you and Chang marry.

WAHLING: Yes, yes. Anything to make you happy.

CHANG: And you would never fight with Li Cha, isn't that right?

WAHLING: No — never again.

LI CHA: We would all become friends.

MANDARIN (*Looking over bridge*): Look! Look! Here they are! Under the bridge!

CHANG (*In normal voice*): Oh-oh!

LI CHA: Come out immediately, Kongshee. (KONGSHEE *and* CHANG *come out from under bridge.*)

WAHLING: Chang—you fooled us. How could you do such a thing?

LI CHA: Bad children!

WAHLING: Don't be too hard on your daughter and Chang. Forgive them.

CHANG: Yes, you said that if we would only return you would allow us to marry.

LI CHA: I did, didn't I?

MANDARIN: But what about our agreement?

LI CHA: My daughter's happiness is more important than our agreement.

MANDARIN (*Angrily*): I will take you to court! This is a

scandal! (DOG *enters, growls, and bites* MANDARIN's *leg. Howling,* MANDARIN *jumps about in confusion. Others laugh.*)
LI CHA (*Picking up* DOG *as* MANDARIN *exits*): No, no. My daughter's happiness comes first. So I will give my blessings to you both. We shall make new wedding plans.
WAHLING: And hold the wedding on the bridge.
CHANG: Yes — our bridge.
KONGSHEE: Our bridge of the Blue Willow. (*Young couple walk to center of bridge as curtain falls.*)

THE END

The Blue Willow

PRODUCTION NOTES

Number of Puppets: 9 hand or rod puppets or marionettes.
Playing Time: 15 minutes.
Costumes: Wahling and Chang are dressed in simple Chinese "pajamas." Kongshee wears more elaborate "pajamas." Li Cha and Mandarin are in long coats and wear pillbox hats. Dog is a little Pekingese. Cat is same size as Dog. Two Bluebirds should look like small puppets on wires.
Properties: None required.
Setting: Scene 1 should look very much like a Blue Willow-pattern plate. Copy the scene and blue coloring from such a dish, showing the two houses, bridge and willow tree, in blue, against a plain, cream-colored background. Scene 2 may be played in front of the curtain, or a Chinese interior may be painted on a drop.
Lighting: Simple, direct light, except for Scene 3, which should be in blues, for an evening effect.
Sound: No special effects. Recorded Chinese music, to set the mood, if desired.

THE RABBIT WHO WANTED RED WINGS

An American folk tale

Characters

STUBBY, *a little rabbit*
MAMA RABBIT, *his mother*
MR. BUSHYTAIL, *a squirrel*
MR. PORCUPINE
MISS PUDDLEDUCK
MR. GROUNDHOG
LITTLE RED BIRD
NARRATOR

SCENE 1

BEFORE RISE: NARRATOR *addresses audience.*

NARRATOR: Once upon a time, there was a little rabbit whose name was Stubby because of the little stubby tail he had. Stubby had beautiful long ears and two bright eyes, four soft little feet and soft, pretty fur — but he wasn't happy. He wanted to be someone else, instead of the nice little rabbit he was.

*   *   *

SETTING: *The forest. At either side of stage are two broad trees, each with a door in it. Mama Rabbit's house is at left, and Mr. Bushytail's house, at right.*

AT RISE: MAMA RABBIT *is sweeping her stoop.* STUBBY *is nearby, playing.*

STUBBY (*Singing to the tune of "Twinkle, Twinkle, Little Star"*):
Wish I were a flower bright,
With petals red that fold at night.
Wish I were a mousie, too,
With softest fur of grayish hue,
Even if I were a lamb —
Anything but what I am . . .
Wish I were a flower bright,
With petals red that fold at night.

MAMA: Now, Stubby. Don't be so unhappy. You are a very handsome little rabbit. Be content to be yourself. (*She exits left into door in tree.*)

STUBBY (*Sighing*): Yes, Mama. . . . (MR. BUSHYTAIL *enters right out of his tree with a basket over his arm.*)

BUSHYTAIL: Good morning there, young man.

STUBBY: Good morning, Mr. Bushytail.

BUSHYTAIL: I see you are up nice and early. Have you been a good rabbit?

STUBBY: Yes, Mr. Bushytail. Where are you going so early in the morning?

BUSHYTAIL: I've got to do my shopping today. The nuts are beginning to fall from the trees now. Have to get ready for the cold months ahead, you know.

STUBBY: That sure is a beautiful bushy tail you have.

BUSHYTAIL: Thank you, Stubby.

STUBBY: I wish I had a tail like yours. It's so big and fluffy.

BUSHYTAIL: Be content with the pretty little one you have. Now, mind your mother. (*He exits left.*)

STUBBY: Goodbye, Mr. Bushytail. (*To himself*) I sure would like a different tail, though. (MR. PORCUPINE *enters right.*)

PORCUPINE: Good morning, Stubby.

STUBBY: Good morning, Mr. Porcupine.

PORCUPINE: Have you been a good boy today?

STUBBY: Oh, yes.

PORCUPINE: Have you been helping your mother?

STUBBY: Whenever I can.

PORCUPINE: That's a good boy.

STUBBY: Where are you going?

PORCUPINE: I'm going to have my quills sharpened.

STUBBY (*Touching* MR. PORCUPINE's *quills*): Ouch!

PORCUPINE: Be careful. They are still quite sharp.

STUBBY: I wish I had long sharp quills on my back.

PORCUPINE: Be content with the beautiful fur you have, Stubby . . . and mind your mother. Good day, Stubby.

STUBBY: Good morning, Mr. Porcupine. (MR. PORCUPINE *exits left.*) I still wish I were a flower or a little gray mouse.

MAMA (*Re-entering from left tree*): Stubby, there you are. Stay near the house now and don't go wandering off.

STUBBY: I will, Mama. (MISS PUDDLEDUCK *waddles on, right, with a basket. She wears red rubbers.*)

MAMA: Good morning, Miss Puddleduck. Where are you going today?

PUDDLEDUCK: Off to visit Auntie Goosey Gander. She's under the weather and so I'm taking her some waterlily soup I made myself. Would you like to taste it, Stubby?

STUBBY: No, thank you, Miss Puddleduck. I've had my breakfast, and besides, I've tasted it before.

PUDDLEDUCK: It's good for you, young man. I must be on my way. Goodbye, Mrs. Rabbit. If you go out, don't forget your umbrella. It might rain.

MAMA: Thank you. Goodbye, Miss Puddleduck. (MISS PUDDLEDUCK *waddles off, left.*)

STUBBY: I wish I had a pair of red rubbers like Miss Puddleduck's.

MAMA: Why don't you go visit old Mr. Groundhog? Perhaps he can put some sense into your little head. (*She exits into house, left.*)

STUBBY: That's just what I'll do. Mr. Groundhog is smarter than anybody. (*He goes off singing to the tune of "Twinkle, Twinkle, Little Star."*) Wish I were a flower bright . . . (*Exits left; curtain*)

* * *

SCENE 2

SETTING: *Mr. Groundhog's home. A "fire" is burning in the fireplace.*

AT RISE: MR. GROUNDHOG *is lounging in a chair. A large armchair is nearby.*

GROUNDHOG (*Singing to the tune of "Pop Goes the Weasel"*):
    It's nice to be a bachelor,
    To live all by myself.
    No need to clean up anything,
    Or put stuff on a shelf.
    Live a life of quiet,
    And there's no need to work —
    That's the life I'm craving for,
    That's what I like. (*Sighs*)
Ahhh. (*Sinks deeper in his chair. Knock on door is heard.*) Who could that be, disturbing me so early in the day? (*Calls*) Come in! (STUBBY *enters.*) Come in, little Stubby. How are you today?

STUBBY: Just fine, Mr. Groundhog.

GROUNDHOG: What do you want of me? You are usually full of questions and desires. What is it today?

STUBBY: Mama said that if I wished for something I should see you, 'cause you're so smart.

GROUNDHOG (*Chuckling*): What do you want, Stubby?

STUBBY: I'd like to have a bushy tail just like Mr. Bushytail — and beautiful quills on my back like Mr. Porcupine — and red rubbers like Miss Puddleduck's.

GROUNDHOG (*Chuckling again*): Why don't you go down to the wishing pond? If you look into the water at yourself and turn in a circle three times, you will get your wish.

STUBBY: Really? How do I get there? I want to go right away.

GROUNDHOG: Right down the path, then left at the big oak tree — you'll find your way easily enough.

STUBBY: I'll leave right away, Mr. Groundhog. Thank you very much.

GROUNDHOG: If you get into any trouble, just come back. But be careful, and use your head.

STUBBY: Goodbye, Mr. Groundhog. (*He exits.*)

GROUNDHOG: Poor little rabbit! He'll be taught his lesson. He'll learn. (*Chuckles again; curtain.*)

*   *   *

SCENE 3

SETTING: *The wishing pond.*

AT RISE: LITTLE RED BIRD *is singing. It flies away as* STUBBY *enters.*

STUBBY: Don't run away, little red bird. (*Sadly*) It's gone. (*Turns*) Here I am, at the wishing pond. It's just where

Mr. Groundhog said it was. (BIRD *flies back, chirping.*)
Now what was I supposed to wish? Hmm. I forgot.
(BIRD *flits about and lands on* STUBBY's *head.* STUBBY
laughs.) What fun. Wouldn't it be great if I could fly like
the pretty red bird? (BIRD *flies about again.*) I know what
I'll wish for! (*Recites*)

> Wishing pond, O wishing pond,
> All blue and clear and bright,
> Grant me my wish I wish,
> Listen to my plight.
> Give me pretty wings of red
> Upon my back and shoulders.
> I'll fly away just like a bird
> Over rocks and boulders.

(*Speaks*) Now I must turn around three times. (*He turns.*)
My back feels funny. Something is happening. (*Red
wings appear on his back. NOTE: Wings may be fastened to
his back quickly from offstage using Velcro or hooks.* BIRD *chirps
loudly.*) Did it work, pretty red bird? I'll look in the
pond. (*He goes to pond.*) It worked! It worked! I have
pretty red wings on my back. Hooray! Now to try them
out. (*He flies.*) I can fly! I can fly! Hooray! (BIRD *squawks
and flies off.*) Wait, little red bird. Don't be afraid. It's
me, Stubby — with new — red — wings. I'll hurry
home to show Mama. (*He flies off. Curtain*)

*   *   *

SCENE 4

SETTING: *Same as Scene 1. Darker background.*
AT RISE: STUBBY *enters right.*

STUBBY: It's getting dark. I shouldn't have stayed away so long. (*He knocks on door of tree, left.*) Mama! Mama! I'm home. Let me in. (MAMA *opens door.*) Let me in, Mama!

MAMA: Who are you?

STUBBY: I'm your little boy, Stubby. Don't you recognize me?

MAMA: You are not my little boy. Stubby doesn't have red wings. In fact, I've never in all my life seen a rabbit with red wings. Get out of here. Go away! (*She slams the door.*)

STUBBY: But, Mama! (*Sound of thunder is heard.*) Oh, dear. She doesn't know who I am. What will I do now? Maybe Mr. Bushytail will let me stay with him. (*Sound of thunder is repeated, followed by rain.*) Oh, my . . . It's starting to rain, too. (*He knocks on* MR. BUSHYTAIL's *door, right.*) Mr. Bushytail. Let me in!

BUSHYTAIL (*Opening door*): Who's there?

STUBBY: I'm Stubby. Don't you recognize me?

BUSHYTAIL: Not with those red wings. You must be a ghost. A rabbit ghost. (*Frightened*) Ohhh! (*He slams the door. Sounds of thunder, rain, are repeated. Flash of lightning is seen.*)

STUBBY: What will I do? (*He starts to cry.* MISS PUDDLEDUCK *hurries in.*)

PUDDLEDUCK: Oh, this rain. Dear, dear. And it's so late.

STUBBY: Miss Puddleduck. Would you help me? (MISS PUDDLEDUCK *sees* STUBBY, *screams and runs off.*) Oh, dear. I've scared her, too. What *will* I do? (*Cries*) I know — I'll go back to see Mr. Groundhog. He'll help me. (*He hurries off. Curtain.*)

*   *   *

Scene 5

SETTING: *Same as Scene 2.*
AT RISE: MR. GROUNDHOG *opens door and looks out. Thunder and rain are heard.*

GROUNDHOG: What a terrible night! (*Closes door. Sounds stop.*) Not fit for bird or beast. I'll just lock up for the night. (*Sound of a knock on the door*) Now, who could that be? Hello, out there! Who is it?
STUBBY (*Calling from offstage*): It's Stubby, Mr. Groundhog. May I come in out of the rain and cold?
GROUNDHOG (*Opening door*): Come in, Stubby.
STUBBY (*Entering*): Thank you ever so much.
GROUNDHOG: Why, look at you, little rabbit. What a wet little bunny you are!
STUBBY: I know. But I can't go home. It's awful — just awful.
GROUNDHOG: What's wrong?
STUBBY: Mama didn't know who I was. Mr. Bushytail didn't know who I was, and Miss Puddleduck ran away from me. It's because of these awful red wings.
GROUNDHOG: Oh — I didn't notice.
STUBBY: What will I do? (*Cries*)
GROUNDHOG: First you'd better get warm and get some sleep. Then in the morning go back to the wishing pond.
STUBBY: Why should I go back to the wishing pond?
GROUNDHOG: To wish *off* your new red wings.
STUBBY (*Settling down by the fire and yawning*): Yes . . . wish off my . . . new . . . red . . . wings. (*Sleeps*)
GROUNDHOG: Poor little fellow. Perhaps now he'll learn his lesson. (MR. GROUNDHOG *covers* STUBBY *with a blanket. Curtain.*)

*   *   *

SCENE 6

SETTING: *Same as Scene 3.*
AT RISE: LITTLE RED BIRD *is flying about, singing.* STUBBY *enters.*

STUBBY: There you are, little red bird. I'm back again. (*Angrily*) You can keep your old red wings! (*Recites to the pond*)

> Wishing pond, O wishing pond,
> I'm here to wish once more.
> Please take away my pretty wings,
> And make me as I was before.
> Just a little rabbit
> And no one else I'll be,
> I'll be content with what I am,
> And I'll be good you'll see.

(*He turns three times, and the wings disappear.* BIRD *sings sweetly.* STUBBY *looks into pond.*) The wings are gone! They are gone! Hooray! I'm a plain little rabbit again. Won't Mama be pleased! Red bird, you can fly all you want. I'll just hop along. (*He hops.*) Hop, hop! Hop, hop! Hop, hop! (*He exits left.*)

MAMA (*Entering right with* MR. BUSHYTAIL, MR. PORCUPINE, *and* MISS PUDDLEDUCK): I'm so glad you came along to help me find my little boy. Where could Stubby be? (*She cries softly.*)

BUSHYTAIL: Now, now. He couldn't have gone too far.

PUDDLEDUCK: Don't cry. We'll find him.

MAMA: But, he is so little! You don't suppose he was caught by that monster we all met last night, do you?

PUDDLEDUCK: What a terrible sight that was. (*Shocked*) A monster with red wings and the head of a rabbit!

PORCUPINE: No, no. I'm sure Stubby is all right. We'll find him.

STUBBY (*Re-entering left*): Mama! Mama! Here I am! (*He hops to* MAMA.)

MAMA (*Hugging* STUBBY): My little rabbit!

STUBBY: And a rabbit I'll stay. No more will I wish to be something or someone else.

BUSHYTAIL: Let's go home.

PUDDLEDUCK: Good idea.

STUBBY: And goodbye forever to you, wishing pond! (*They all laugh and exit. Curtain.*)

THE END

The Rabbit Who Wanted Red Wings

Production Notes

Number of Puppets: 7 marionettes, hand puppets, or rod
puppets. Marionette is preferable for Stubby in order
for him to "fly." Hand puppets and rod puppets can
also be used for "flying," by extending the arm covering on the bottom of the puppet. The bird should always
be a rod puppet, controlled from either above or below
stage.

Playing Time: 15 minutes.

Costumes: Stubby, a rabbit, wears overalls and shirt. He
has a tail that sticks out of his overalls. Mama Rabbit
has a pretty dress and apron with a mob cap on her
head. Mr. Bushytail can be in trousers and jacket. He
has a big, bushy tail that sticks out of his trousers, extending behind his head. Mr. Porcupine is in overalls
and a straw hat. His back consists of quills made from
many light wooden sticks glued in a piece of foam
rubber and attached to his back. Miss Puddleduck is in
a dress, sun bonnet and red rubbers. Mr. Groundhog
is in his shirtsleeves, vest, and trousers. The wings of
Little Red Bird should be loose so they flap when it flies.
Stubby has bright red wings, as indicated in text. If he
is a marionette, string the wings onto his shoulders and
drop them from above where they have been hooked
onto his control. If he is a rod puppet, attach the wings
to his back with Velcro or hooks.

Properties: Broom; baskets, covered for Miss Puddleduck,
closed for Mr. Bushytail; blanket.

Setting: Scene 1, the forest, consisting of two big trees with
working doors which can slam. There is a light back-

ground. For Scene 4, pull a dark cloth across the background. Scene 2, Mr. Groundhog's house, a fireplace, a big armchair, and background. A working door that opens and closes is optional. Scene 3, the wishing pond, a row of pussy willows, with a sign that reads, WISHING POND.

Lighting: Flash of lightning, as indicated in text.

Sound: Thunder; rain; knock on door; cries of bird; as indicated in text.